21st-Century
Dad

A New Father's
Game Plan
to Child Rearing
Conception through Age 2

by Dr. Douglas DeMichele, father of two

Library of Congress Cataloging-in-Publication Data

21st-Century Dad:
A New Father's Game Plan for Child Rearing (conception through age 2)
ISBN   0-9673677-0-0

Copyright © 1999 by Douglas DeMichele
J.C.P.D. Inc.
PO Box 13884
Gainesville, FL 32604

Printed in the USA by Tompson-Shore, Inc.

ISBN   0-9673677-0-0

Dedicated to my Family

21st-
Century
Dad

Contents

21st-Century Dad

21st-Century Dad

Acknowledgments

Several people have contributed to the development and implementation of the **21st-Century Dad**. As this first edition goes to press, the author would like to thank:

- his wife, Pamela, for her relentless support and encouragement of the book. She provided the first review of each topic and was instrumental in providing details to help the reader understand a mother's perspective;

- our kids, Jana and Chase, who provided the true-life experiences and brought to light the topics discussed in this book;

- our editor, Patricia Bates McGhee, for her support and the messaging of the content to make for easy reading;

- our graphic design professional, Sharon LaFragola, for the layout and cover design;

- our photographer, Ray Feinberg (grandpa), for the photography;

- our parents, for their leadership and guidance during the child-rearing phases of our kids' lives;

- our extended families for their encouragement; and

- Dr. Pini Orbach, for the book endorsement.

21st-
Century
Dad

Introduction

Since you are reading this page, I presume you have just become or will soon become what I call a 21st-Century Dad. Congratulations! The experiences you are about to enjoy are priceless and will touch you in every way. Try to savor every moment because the time will pass by quickly.

As a recent father myself, I quickly found out that almost all of today's childhood development books are written for Parents or for Mom alone. This book, however, is for you — the 21st-Century Dad. It addresses the Dads of the world and how Dads relate with Moms during pregnancy, birth and child rearing. It also provides real-life examples of situations and environmental changes that you — the 21st-Century Dad — should expect.

This edition highlights personal circumstances that you and Mom will face from Baby's conception through age 2. Hopefully, the stories and topics shared will help you become a more informed Dad and reassure you that you are not the first male to fear the Dad role or to be placed in situations you've never experienced before. You will be introduced to several aspects of fatherhood that will re-define your relationships with friends and relatives and, of course, alter your own lifestyle. After studying this game plan, you should recognize the meaning of the word "Dad" and be well on your way to the positive development and nurturing of Baby as well as the continued development of your personal relationship with Mom.

Of course, all family situations are different. Some Dads live with Baby's Mom, and others do not. Some Dads may raise Baby alone, too. The scenarios presented in this book are from my own

21st-Century Dad

experience and parallel the husband-and-wife situation but can be easily adjusted to fit your own situation. Also, becoming a Dad may be a planned or unplanned event. If you unexpectedly find out that you're becoming a Dad – or have recently been informed that your adopted Baby will arrive soon — you too can benefit from the topics shared in this book. And, if you find out that multiple births (twins, triplets, etc.) are in your future, you may have to make adjustments above and beyond those noted here.

A personal note for you, 21st-Century Dad. Although this book is not as detailed — or as long — as many child-rearing guides on the market, the practical topics and real-life photos should help you become a more informed Dad. I remember being in your shoes and wondering how my life was going to change when we became pregnant. Even though friends shared their personal stories with me, most of my information came from Mom, an 8-week hospital prenatal class or excerpts from the maternal books Mom encouraged me to read. While some of the books were interesting and excellent resources early on, not one gave me a real-life perspective of how Baby would affect *my* life. This book is written to provide that perspective – and offer a game plan for dealing with these changes — in a concise, yet informative fashion.

How To Use This Book

This book's two sections — Conception through Birth and Birth through Age 2 — as well as its table of contents, glossary and three appendices are designed to help you quickly reference topics of interest. While the book's goal is to make you more informed as a 21st-Century Dad, your personal situation will influence the way you fulfill your role as a father. Okay, 21st-Century Dad, here we go.

21st-
Century
Dad

Foreword

Although there are countless examples of what becoming a Dad might mean to you and other Dads, there are a few commonalities as well. The following list is a collection of comments I've heard from Dads I've known through the years:

• Becoming a Dad is extremely exciting

• Becoming a Dad gives you a feeling of strength and self-worth

• Procreation is a natural phenomenon

• You are the "fun" Parent in the relationship

• You have the opportunity to share your personal beliefs and values with your Child

• You have added responsibilities:
   Life insurance
   Home security
   Family security
   Future educational opportunities for your Child
   Being available for your Child on your Child's terms and not yours·
   Being available for Mom as needed to help your Family
   Resources to feed, clothe and nurture the Child and Family

• Baby will say your name first — even though "Da" is one of the first sounds Baby can produce, you will beam when you hear what you believe is "Dad"

21st-Century Dad

Change Begins

Becoming a Dad will, indeed, change your life.

All of the above are true. Becoming a Dad will, indeed, change your life. But the intrinsic rewards you reap from Baby can be harnessed only through the special bond you develop. Sure, you may feel overwhelmed at times, but be patient and find good in every situation. Moms have traditionally fulfilled the role of nurturer in society, but now you can seize this unique opportunity to mold your beautiful Baby into a young Child who carries on your traditions and values. Take time to enjoy each stage of Baby's development — especially in the first 2 years — because they are priceless and will pass quickly.

1

Chapter 1 -
You Find Out You're Pregnant

The first step toward becoming a good Dad is realizing that as soon as you learn Mom is pregnant, **you** are also pregnant. Your role as Dad has begun. Like most people who are trying to have a child, you will be proud and feel a sense of accomplishment. You and Mom will begin discussing topics you've heard only on talk shows – topics like:

Pregnancy

*The first step toward becoming a good Dad is realizing that as soon as you learn Mom is pregnant, **you** are also pregnant.*

- The Child's and Family's financial future
- Baby's name
- Baby's appearance
- Whether or not your present home will be big enough
- Using day care or staying home with Baby and, of course,
- Whether Baby will be a boy or a girl

Like many Dads, you will second-guess your desire to change your controlled life and start a Family in an uncontrolled environment. This decision may have been conscious when you and Mom discussed having a Family, but I assure you, this game plan introduces topics that you and Mom have not yet discussed. As you review the chapters, take time to discuss these topics at length because they pose real-life situations and influence decisions you and Mom will face in the next 3 years. Understanding and

21st-Century Dad

recognizing these topics can improve the health and well-being of your young Family. Yes, Dad, you are now a Family man!

Like most new Moms in their first pregnancy, your wife/partner will read every childhood book she can find. She will talk with friends and family members who have children. She will ask you a thousand questions — at least. This behavior is normal and actually healthy for your relationship.

However, you must understand that a pregnant Mom and a pregnant Dad are light-years apart. While pregnant Moms experience hormonal changes from the very beginning of the first trimester (or first 3 months) of pregnancy, pregnant Dads continue to live life as they did before.

Your friends who have pregnant wives will often share stories about their wives complaining, tossing their cookies, suffering mood swings all the time and, in general, being drastically different than before they got pregnant. New Dads find it normal to vent and express frustrations with friends, but we must remember that, as Dads, we are pregnant only at home in the evenings. Moms, however, are pregnant 24 hours a day, 7 days a week for at least 9 months. We, on the other hand, can go on with life, work and exercise at the same level and intensity as we did before, fully knowing that our bodies will not change. Our clothes won't become too small, we won't feel nauseous or become sick on a regular basis, we won't get hemorrhoids or varicose veins, our boobs won't swell and, of course, we won't have to pee every 10 minutes and we can still have a beer anytime we like. Let's face it, becoming a pregnant Dad is cake compared to the life alterations Mom will experience over the 9-month period. You, as Mom will remind you, are the lucky one.

Talking Trash

New Dads find it normal to vent and express frustrations with friends.

The First 3 Months

No matter how excited you and Mom are about Baby's arrival, she will constantly let you know she is carrying the greater share of the load during pregnancy, and she is right. As a team, however, you and Mom will face critical decisions about Baby's — and the Family's — future. You will likely voice your opinion in most cases. However, ultimately, Mom will have the responsibility to finalize many decisions.

The first decision is selecting an obstetrician (OB doctor). Mom must find a physician whom she is comfortable with and one who is listed on your insurance plan. (Selecting a midwife and/or birthing coach, should you desire one, is also an option.) Once the doctor is selected and the initial pregnancy visit has been completed, I encourage you to attend as many doctor's visits as possible. Not only will you receive firsthand information from the doctor, but Mom will know you are excited about the pregnancy. The excuse "I have to work" is lame and unacceptable. It will not work when Baby is 2 years old and sick, so it shouldn't be used during pregnancy, either. Murphy's Law will hold true during the first visit you fail to attend. The doctor will present an issue Mom would prefer you hear together. So, if at all possible, accompany Mom, even for the 10-minute visits.

Moms Over 35

If Mom is over 35, she will experience stress above and beyond that of a younger Mom because the probability of complications increases with Mom's age. If this is the case in your situation, show extra compassion and read up on later-life pregnancy.

Moms in the over-35 age bracket are encouraged to have additional tests, such as amniocentesis. Regardless of your feelings about advanced medicine, anticipate friends and the doctor to pressure her to have these tests. Before Mom agrees, learn the facts about the tests from reputable sources — research the Internet and ask your doctor for a professional opinion.

Did you know that one in 200 pregnancies miscarries as a result of the amniocentesis test (*Williams Obstetrics*, 1997)? If you and Mom

The Quarterback

Ultimately, Mom will have the responsibility to finalize many decisions.

have decided that terminating the pregnancy is not a choice you would make, you may consider placing Baby's well-being in God's hands. Knowing in advance that Baby may have complications or even Down's syndrome will certainly "prepare" you for the news when Baby arrives, but it is not going to change the outcome and may exponentially increase stress in your relationship prior to Baby's birth.

You should also confer with the doctor to learn more about the possibility of receiving a false positive on the tri-screen test that pregnant Moms of all ages are encouraged to take, and then determine whether or not the test is right for you. I have known several couples who have stressed out for weeks because the tri-screen revealed a positive result, indicating a problem, when in fact the results were incorrect and Baby was perfect. If, after careful research, you and Mom determine the tests are necessary, proceed with the advice of your doctor.

Alcohol, Tobacco and Caffeine

The issue of using alcohol and tobacco during pregnancy is a concern for many Dads, as well as Moms, because the doctor will instruct Mom to abstain from these products. If you smoke, do not smoke in your home or around Mom. If you drink, decide whether you will drink in front of Mom or abstain, as well. Many pregnant Dads think this time period is excellent because Mom is the designated driver and they can get smashed when they choose. WRONG! Although this may be the case on one or possibly two occasions, when Baby arrives you will need to be a responsible Dad and consider Baby's safety. Of course, the decision to consume alcohol is a personal one. But, during pregnancy Mom may appreciate it if you avoid drinking more than a casual beverage (beer, wine). Once Baby arrives, you certainly cannot be inebriated during a 2 a.m. diaper change. And you never want to deal with an accident that occurred because you were drinking.

Pre-Game Party

Mom is the designated driver ... WRONG!

In addition to restricting alcohol and tobacco use, several research studies recommend that Moms avoid caffeine during pregnancy. Once again, if you can help Mom by altering your consumption of caffeine products, she will be more successful in modifying her intake.

Diet

One of the most difficult topics you and Mom will face during pregnancy is the Family's daily diet. Mom will most likely adjust her eating habits at the advice of her doctor, and you will be the recipient of the changes. The doctor will encourage Mom to eat more fruit and vegetables, milk and milk products, iron-rich foods (good for meat-eaters), natural juices and natural foods and fewer chemical sweeteners and empty-calorie foods. (By the way, empty-calorie foods are the good ones – you know, alcohol, soft drinks, sweets and most munchies.)

Undoubtedly, you'll have to decide what to eat while Mom is pregnant. Most likely you'll give in and eat the doctor-recommended meals. Or, you may opt to tell Mom it really doesn't matter what she eats — just look at So & So. Whatever you decide, keep in mind that Baby's health is influenced by diet.

The likelihood that Mom follows the doctor's dietary recommendations is influenced by your willingness to modify your diet. Most Dads attest to modifying their diets in the household and then sneaking favorite foods while at work. Just remember, Mom can't do this because she is pregnant 24 hours a day, 7 days a week for at least 9 months. The greatest benefit of modifying your diet is that Mom will be less likely to harass you and give you a hard time.

Weight Gain

Another topic pregnant Moms are concerned about is their weight. Typically, they ask:

• How much weight should I gain?

• What will I do after pregnancy to get the weight off if I become obese?

• Will Dad still find me attractive when I am fat and flabby?

Mom will tell you that So & So became huge after her pregnancy so her husband is no longer interested in her. These issues are real, and everyone will address them differently. However, as a 21st-Century Dad, you need to reassure Mom that you understand what she is experiencing and will support and love her through pregnancy

The Sneak

Most Dads attest to modifying their diets in the household and then sneaking favorite foods while at work.

and afterward. If her weight gain becomes excessive, the doctor will help her control it through proper diet and exercise programs. The average weight gain is between 25 and 35 pounds, with small-framed petite women on the low end of the range and larger-boned women at the high end.

According to the 20th edition of *Williams Obstetrics* (1997), the approximate breakdown for weight gain is:

> 6 to 8 pounds for Baby
> 1.5 pounds for the placenta
> 1.75 pounds for the amniotic fluid
> 2 pounds for uterine enlargement
> 1 pound for breast tissue
> 7 pounds for fat
> 2.75 pounds for blood volume
> 3 pounds for fluid in tissue

Mom should anticipate a weight gain of 3 to 4 pounds during the first trimester, 12 to 14 pounds during the second trimester and 1 pound per week during the 7th and 8th months.

Ultrasound

Ultrasound can help the obstetrician determine how many fetuses there are, if the fetus is healthy, the size and position of the fetus and, in general, exactly how the pregnancy is progressing. Depending on the individual pregnancy, ultrasound can be done any time from the 5th week of pregnancy through delivery. For a "normal" pregnancy, ultrasound is not done until the 21st week.

The ultrasound appointment is usually the "premier" visit for most parents. Mom and Dad are excited about the ultrasound because they have the opportunity to actually see the surprisingly well-formed fetus. Within a few seconds of the exam you will reaffirm that Mom is, indeed, pregnant and that you are a Dad. You will see the fetus for the first time and see features such as hands, feet, face and limbs. Additionally, you will witness firsthand the functioning of the heart and lungs. Most ultrasound technicians will give you a few pictures to take home, and some encourage you to bring a videotape to record the entire procedure.

Preview of Game Film

Within a few seconds of the exam you will reaffirm that Mom is, indeed, pregnant and that you are a Dad.

Prior to the exam you and Mom will have discussed the issue of determining Baby's sex during ultrasound. Many Parents want to know the sex so they can prepare Baby's room, name Baby and determine color schemes for Baby's clothing. Others prefer to keep the sex a secret until D-day (delivery day). Most likely, the technician will ask you before the exam if you want to know the sex and then do everything possible to accommodate your request.

Although determining Baby's sex can be exciting, observing the heart and lungs in action, finding out that measurements of the limbs and head are in the proper range and seeing Baby move make the visit an awesome experience. Following the ultrasound appointment, your compassion for Mom and her hormonal adjustments may improve. When Mom says Baby just kicked her, you can visualize what has happened. When she says "I have to pee," you may understand that her bladder is being constricted. And when she says "I am hungry," you may be more willing to go out for ice cream during the "big game" or on a cold evening. Remember, during this stage of pregnancy you can expect Mom to keep your home cold, even though you may be freezing.

Emergency Phone Numbers

During pregnancy, establish a phone list for quick reference in case anything goes wrong before the birth. The list should include the:

- primary physician

- poison control center

- hospital

- work and cell phone numbers, if appropriate, and

- a few close friends and relatives

Although friends and relatives will most likely be called after Baby is born, in the event Mom is unable to reach you at work or on your cell phone or beeper (if you have them), it's reassuring to know that someone is available to transport Mom to the hospital, should an emergency occur.

21st-Century Dad

Child Development Books/Articles

Hopefully, this book will help you better understand your role as Dad and husband/partner prior to Baby's birth. However, learn as much as you can through a variety of sources. Becoming educated in child rearing is labor-intensive (no pun intended) and hard work. But, when the knowledge you gain can be applied directly to your Family, the time investment is well worth it. Read as much as possible to become more familiar with infants, toddlers and Mom's changing body. If you take your research seriously, you will be better informed to make decisions as a 21st-Century Dad. Additionally, a greater understanding of Mom's world and her ever-changing body may help you cope with the emotional fluctuations common during pregnancy.

2

Chapter 2 –
Getting Ready for Baby's Arrival

Stuff You'll Need

You and Mom need to be on the same page when it comes to purchasing items to care for Baby. This decision is, of course, personal and depends on your Family's socioeconomic status and gifts you receive to get your Family started. One Mom and Dad may believe certain items are vital to nurturing Baby. Another couple may believe the same items are frivolous and unnecessary. Your friends and relatives also will influence the conversations you and Mom have concerning what is necessary.

The following two categories will help you determine whether or not you need certain items to care for Baby. Category 1 items are rated as a "Must" – they should be purchased to help Dad, Mom and Baby enjoy the experience. Category 2 items are rated as "Highly Useful" — they may be useful for your particular situation. Although the items listed in this chapter are commonly discussed by new Parents, only you and Mom can evaluate the importance of the items and decide which specific items MUST be purchased prior to Baby's arrival.

Detailed descriptions of the items, their special features and appropriate prices and when you will use them are found in Appendix A ("Must Haves") and Appendix B ("Highly Useful").

For quick reference, the item, its cost and approximate time used are provided for each category in the summaries below. To anticipate how much you can expect to spend, price per item is listed as modest (the low end of the range) or extravagant (the upper end of the range). Prices are estimates only and may be higher or lower in your area of the country.

Summary of Anticipated "Must" Items

Item	Modest Cost	Extravagant Cost	Time Used
Changing table	$ 60	$100	Birth - potty training
Changing pad	4	20	Birth - potty training
Crib	100	500	Birth - toddler bed
Mattress	30	100	Birth - toddler bed
Mattress cover/ liner pad	12	15	Birth - toddler bed
Sheets/blankets	8	15	Birth - toddler bed
Stroller, full-size	40	160	2 weeks - 4 years
Stroller, umbrella	25	30	2 months - 4 years
Lotion	2	14	Birth - adult life
Diaper bags	10	35	Birth - potty training
Petroleum jelly	2	3	Birth - adult life
Rubbing alcohol, cotton swabs	1	2	Birth - adult life
Wet wipes	3	6	Birth - adult life
Sunscreen	7	15	6 months - adult life
Diaper-rash cream	2	4	Birth - potty training
Bathing items (washcloth, towel)	6	10	Birth - toddler
Portable bathtub	10	20	Birth - toddler
Infant car seat/carrier	40	60	Birth - 1 year
Toddler car seat	40	85	1 year - 3 years
Stain remover	4	7	Birth - adult life
Bib	2	8	Birth - toddler
Baby shampoo	2	8	Birth - toddler
Baby soap	2	8	Birth - toddler
Nursing pads (if breast-feeding)	3	10	Birth - 1 to 2 years
Nurse kit	8	10	Birth - adult life
(thermometer, suction bulb, medicine syringe, nail clippers)			
Burp cloth, 3-pack	3	5	Birth - toddler
Bottle washer	2	3	Birth - 1.5 years
Bottle dry rack	3	5	Birth - 1.5 years
Bottles	1	4	Birth - 1 year
Nipples	2	5	Birth - 1 year
Formula (case)	25	60	Birth - 1 year
Diapers	20	60	Birth - potty training
(average month's supply)			
Clothes based on Baby's size			
Undergarments, 3-pack	6	9	
Sleeper	10	20	
Hats	2	40	
Shoes	6	50	
Socks	4	10	
TOTAL	$507	$1,516	

Summary of Anticipated "Highly Useful" Items

Item	Modest Cost	Extravagant Cost	Time Used
Wet-wipe warmer	$ 12	$ 22	Birth - potty training
Portable crib	80	120	Birth - toddler
Mobiles	20	80	Birth - 9 months
Crib side pads/quilt	40	60	Birth - toddler bed
Baby stabilizers	15	17	Birth - infancy
Diaper stacker	10	30	Birth - potty training
Bouncer	20	40	Birth - 6 months
Sling	20	50	Birth - 10 months
Vaporizer	12	30	Birth - adult life
Automatic baby swing	40	120	2 weeks - 9 months
Pacifier	1	3	Birth - 2 years
Baby monitor	20	150	Birth - Mom and Dad grow out of it
Activity board	10	25	6 months - toddler sleeps in a bed
Chest/backpack baby carrier	15	80	2 months - 18 months
Auto mirror	3	5	Birth - toddler
Sunshade	5	7	Birth - adult life
Medical supplies Acetaminophen	4	8	Birth - toddler
Ibuprofen	4	8	Birth - toddler
Saltwater drops	3	5	Birth - toddler
Eucalyptus rub	3	6	Birth - adult
Simethicone anti-gas drops	4	8	Birth - end of bottle feeding
Spill-proof cup	3	6	10 months - toddler
Food/bottle storage turntable for cabinet	15	30	Birth - 2 years
Camera	5	500+	Birth - adult life
Video recorder	350	600+	Birth - adult life
TOTAL	$714	$2,010	

Before you purchase that first item, be aware that friends and families commonly share child-care items and many people want to give you a baby shower gift. Many couples shop garage and yard sales to reduce initial expenses, while others purchase all new items. Whether you decide on new or used child-care items, start your planning early.

21st-Century Dad

Most new Parents are unfamiliar with the prices of baby items and can be taken advantage of.

I encourage you and Mom to visit a few department or baby stores and register for the items you would like to have. Although it may seem forward, friends and family will appreciate it and, in turn, buy you what you want rather than guess what you might like. Even though an item you want may cost more than $100, register for it in case a few friends want to go in together on a gift. Select the specific item by number, style and color as there are so many to choose from.

Most new Parents are unfamiliar with the prices of baby items and can be taken advantage of by effective marketing schemes and creative advertising. Take time to educate yourself and avoid being taken to the cleaners because you do not know how much baby-care items really cost. Understand exactly how much extra you are paying for the bells and whistles common in many baby items. Just like shopping for a car or clothing, you get more for your money when you shop around and avoid impulse buying. Informed buyers know the differences between manufacturers and are more likely to make informed decisions in purchases.

Regardless of your preferences, always consider safety and convenience. You don't want to look back and wish you had spent the extra $10 for a particular feature or, even more importantly, risk injury to Baby because you wanted to save a few bucks by purchasing a generic item. The best strategy for deciding which brands to purchase and which to avoid is to ask friends with children and read about the products. To avoid being the victim of sleek marketing strategies and glitzy packaging, focus on product function and not appearance. The Internet is an excellent resource to help you and Mom research products on the market.

Before you fork out the money to buy a product:

- Ask someone (friend, relative) who can endorse the product

- Determine how heavy the product is and how easily you can load it into your vehicle

- Find out if the product is easy to use and if it's Baby-friendly — that is, comfortable for Baby

- Determine how durable and sturdy the product is, especially if you plan to have additional children, and

- Make sure the product is easy to clean, disassemble and re-assemble

Almost all baby items come in a variety of colors and types of materials. They may be pink and frilly or blue and manly. However, if you plan to re-use them for next Baby, consider a unisex style. Some products are durable, some are easy to clean and some look much better than others. Nevertheless, when you make the initial purchase, consider these variables and determine how long you intend to use the item. For example, you may prefer white or light-colored sheets because they're easy to clean and bleach but you might want to avoid a light-colored diaper bag, stroller or car seat. Multi-colored items hide stains and spills better than solids and often stay newer-looking for a longer time.

Again, take time to visit several department or baby stores and register for specific items. Otherwise, you could end up with five crib pads and three mobiles and then have to explain to friends why you returned their gifts.

Decorating "The Room"

In anticipation of Baby's arrival, you and Mom may discuss where to put the crib and what theme is appropriate for Baby's bedroom. If you know Baby's sex from ultrasound or amniocentesis, you may choose a theme and color scheme more representative of Baby's gender. You may want to use popular cartoon characters, teddy bears, a purple dinosaur, a yellow bear or a host of other ideas. Most Dads I have talked to really don't care about color or scheme. They're more concerned about how long it'll take to paint the walls and stencils, hang borders and move furniture.

During the nesting stage (cleaning, reorganizing) of Mom's pregnancy, preparing Baby's bedroom becomes a critical task for Dads. In our household, nesting was taken a step further — we painted every wall in the house, every piece of trim and even changed the carpet throughout the house before Baby's arrival. As

Preparing The Room

Most Dads are concerned about how long it'll take to paint the walls and stencils, hang borders and move furniture.

a 21st-Century Dad, expect to spend at least five weekends cleaning, painting and repairing items around the house.

Naming Baby

One of the responsibilities of being a Parent is deciding what your Child will be named for at least 18 years and probably the rest of life. If Baby is a boy, you may consider a junior or use your name as his middle name. Family traditions, personal circumstances and your interactions with people who have names you like or dislike will influence your naming strategy.

In my experience, Dads have more of an influence on Baby's name than they do in purchasing baby items or designing Baby's bedroom. Most likely, you and Mom will look through several name books, write down 10 or 12 names you like and then discuss possible names for Baby. Be sure to consider Baby's initials to make sure they do not spell anything inappropriate. Additionally, consider the spelling of the name, famous people with that name and anticipate the difficulty your Child will have saying or writing the name in school. Nowadays, any word, activity or location can be used for a name. As Parent, look ahead and anticipate whether or not your Child will be proud of the name or upset with it as a teenager. Naming Baby is exciting and one of the privileges of being a Parent, so have fun with it.

Nicknaming Baby

Parents often have a secondary (or pet) name for Baby. Little girls might be called Angel, Sunshine, Precious or Goldilocks. Little boys might be called Buddy, Champ, Chip or Buster. No matter what you nickname Baby, remember that some pet names stick and continue to be used later in life. Again, as Parent, you have the responsibility to keep Baby from being ridiculed later in life as a result of a pet name.

Traveling

In the early stages of pregnancy and through the 6th month, Mom can travel if she has the energy and feels up to it (assuming no health or pregnancy problems). However, as she approaches the due date, you should plan road trips and air travel only after con-

Baby's Name

Dads have more of an influence on Baby's name than they do in purchasing baby items or designing Baby's bedroom.

sulting with the obstetrician. If possible, plan your business trips far in advance rather than closer to the due date to avoid sensitive issues at work and at home. If plans involve Mom traveling, note that some airlines — in the interest of safety — do not allow pregnant passengers who appear ready to deliver to fly, or else require a letter from the doctor before Mom can board. Talk with your doctor and determine length of trip and visit and how many miles in a vehicle or how many hours in a plane Mom may travel in the last few months.

Prenatal Classes

A 21st-Century Dad should expect to have a conversation about enrolling in a prenatal class. Some Dads want to participate in these classes, and others think that Moms might need them but Dads really don't. Whatever your position, I encourage you to learn more about the different types of classes offered in your area.

For our first Baby I have to admit I was skeptical about the classes prior to enrolling, but I ended up really enjoying the experience. For 8 consecutive weeks, beginning around the 7th month of pregnancy, Mom and I attended 2-hour weekly sessions. The class instructor, a delivery nurse who specialized in prenatal care, continuously shared real-life experiences. I was uncomfortable the first few times, but all the other Dads in the room felt the same way. Some were young, most were married and all of them were glad Mom — and not them — was having Baby. Here's what prenatal classes did for me and might do for you:

- Help Mom realize she isn't the only one dealing with pregnancy's side effects and allow her to meet other Moms suffering from many of the same ailments

- Help you, Dad, understand your role in the delivery room (if you decide to be there)

- Explain the lingo you can expect to hear on delivery day

- Show you what you can expect to experience (through videos)

Scheduling Away Games

Plan your business trips far in advance rather than closer to the due date to avoid sensitive issues at work and at home.

21st-Century Dad

The Minivan Conversation

All 21st-Century Dads and Moms inevitably have "the minivan conversation." Whether the conversation occurs prior to or after Baby's arrival, it will happen. Every couple discusses purchasing a minivan.

When it comes to minivans, there are three types of couples:

- Those who believe the minivan is the greatest vehicle ever designed

- Those who said they would never own a minivan and end up buying one due to pressure from friends and relatives and

- Those who will never own a minivan, no matter what

As a new Parent, expect friends and relatives to ask you when you are going to purchase the minivan. It seems to parallel marriage and children. People who are married want everyone to be married, and people who have children believe everyone should have kids. It's kind of like a club. All minivan users want their friends to join the ranks of the minivan clan. Most Dads who do have minivans claim the vehicle is Mom's and tend to sidestep or downplay the topic.

If a minivan is your thing, go for it. But, a four-door car with a large trunk or a sport-utility vehicle may also accommodate your transportation needs.

Chapter 3 – Off to the Hospital

Most doctors advise Moms to go to the hospital when their water breaks or when their contractions are consistently 3 to 5 minutes apart and so painful Mom can't stand it. This is a stressful time for the first-time Mom and Dad because they are both new to the birthing process and want to avoid being overly exuberant Parents who will be sent home and told Mom is in false labor. When Mom says "Honey, I think it is time," you will probably respond with a "Yeah, right" or "Are you sure?" initially. But when you look into her eyes and see that she is serious, your heart may begin to pound and you may become frantic.

Hopefully, the overnight bag has been pre-packed and is ready to load. This bag should have a change of your clothes, Mom's clothes and clothes/blankets for Baby. Additionally, you probably will want to bring a camera, video camera, phone numbers of friends and family, snacks and any propaganda Mom has determined important for delivery. A final and vital item you must have is the infant car seat. Hospital personnel will examine the car seat to ensure that Baby will be properly secured before you leave the hospital.

Once you and Mom arrive at the hospital and the triage staff confirms that Mom is in true labor (has dilated a few centimeters), you are in for the ride of your life, Dad. The labor may last for an hour or two or from one day to the next. I'm sure your friends

Pre-Game Butterflies

Contractions are consistently 3 to 5 minutes apart and so painful Mom can't stand it.

21st-Century Dad

A 21st-Century Dad commonly participates in the entire birthing process.

have shared their stories and you have read about what to expect, but you have no idea until you experience an entire birth with Mom. In the old days, Dads said "Good luck, Honey" as Moms were sent to the delivery room. Not today. A 21st-Century Dad commonly participates in the entire birthing process.

If Mom is scheduled for a cesarean section due to complications during pregnancy, you will be invited to be by her side in the operating room. If she is able to give birth the natural way, you will be invited to be at her side throughout the process. Most 21st-Century Dads choose to be close to Mom, and I endorse that strategy. Personally, I hate hospitals and tend to feel faint when exposed to blood and gore. Nevertheless, I am glad to say that when my children were born — one by cesarean section and the other naturally — I could only think about the miracle I was witnessing rather than my fear of the environment. When the doctor said, "Dad, here's your baby. Would you like to hold him?," it created an image and moment I will never forget. The entire birthing experience should bring you and Mom closer together as a couple and most likely make you more empathetic to her following delivery. If you're lucky, Mom won't call you every name in the book when she is the final stages of delivery (which is like passing a basketball through an opening the size of the anus). But, if she does, you can understand why.

Baby's Arrival

Now that Baby has arrived and Mom is physically exhausted, you become the gatekeeper – that is, you control the number of phone calls and visitors to her room. Most friends and family members who have had children will understand that Mom needs a few hours of peace and quiet. But if they don't, it is your job to educate them.

You and Mom owe it to yourselves – and to Baby — to spend a few hours with Baby before non-family visitors arrive. This is when a special Family bond may develop between Dad, Mom and Baby. Most likely, you will be glowing and on top of the world, so enjoy it.

After some time passes and visitors come to congratulate you and Mom, be cautious and try to limit their physical interaction with Baby. Of course, immediate relatives should be permitted to hold and cuddle Baby, but friends and acquaintances really should not touch Baby too much at this time. Furthermore, you should be aware that Mom might demonstrate, in the next few weeks and months, emotions that are difficult for you to understand. She might cry for no reason, make comments that she is not ready, capable or worthy to be a Mom, or even appear non-excited about Baby. These emotions are normal and reflect the hormonal changes Mom is experiencing. Be strong and supportive and let her know she is a fantastic wife/partner and Mom, and the maternal instinct will eventually kick in. If she gets worse, or you feel she cannot care for Baby at this time, do not hesitate to seek professional help. This is a rare occurrence but a possibility, nonetheless.

While in the hospital, listen to the doctor, ask the nurses questions and watch the educational videos about child rearing and child development. The more you learn and the more you know, the better you'll be able to help at home.

When you leave the hospital you will need to have the infant car seat (with neck support pad) in the car and know how to secure Baby in it. To properly secure Baby, place Baby in the seat, cross the straps over Baby's chest and secure the strap base. The movable clasp should be adjusted so that it is approximately 2 inches from the neck and has no more than a half inch of slack (which is just about enough space for your fingers to fit underneath). Remember, the car seat should be firmly secured (attached with car restraint) in the back seat, with Baby facing the rear of the vehicle (see manufacturer's directions).

Time For A Pep Talk

Mom might cry for no reason, make comments that she is not ready, capable or worthy to be a Mom, or even appear non-excited about Baby.

For children up to 1 year or 20 pounds.

For children up to 40 pounds.

For children 30-60 pounds.

See manufacturer's instructions.

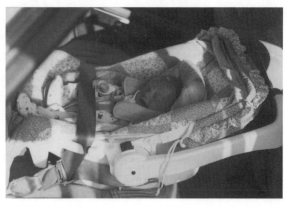

As you drive away from the hospital you may realize that driving a car with Baby inside takes on a whole new perspective. You may find yourself being more cautious than before. You may have overwhelming feelings about Baby facing this big bad world and counting on you for nurturing, care and education. This is a scary time but eventually you will stick out your chest and realize that caring for your Family (Mom and Baby) is the best and most important responsibility of your life.

Baby and Pets

If you have a family dog or cat, you may want to take a baby blanket from the hospital (with Baby's scent on it) home with you before Baby arrives. Some animals take to infants, and others do not. I'm sure you have heard both positive and tragic stories about pets and babies, but when it is your baby, you will take time to look at your particular situation.

When Baby arrives, be sure to give extra attention to the dog or cat so they do not become jealous of the new addition. Mom will be busy and tired, so this responsibility and all other pet-related duties fall in your lap.

First Week Home — What Do You Do?

My advice to you is to take at least a week off work to be a full-time Dad and nursemaid for Mom. Parents and in-laws can provide emotional support and comfort if they live in town but, during the first week, I encourage you to give parenting a try on your own. Save additional assistance from family and friends for the next few weeks when you return to work.

The first few weeks are extremely difficult — and even testy — for most new Parents. Baby will keep you awake and need to be fed

Who Needs Sleep?

Baby will keep you awake and need to be fed every 2 to 3 hours, 24 hours a day.

36

every 2 to 3 hours, 24 hours a day. Mom will be sore from delivery and need constant assistance, and your daily chores will be doubled (yours plus hers). You will be doing the grocery shopping. You will be cleaning the bottles and making the formula (for formula-fed babies) or you may be cleaning the breast pump accessories (for breast-fed babies) after each feeding or pumping. If Mom is fatigued from delivery and/or sleep deprived, expect to become the bathing expert, the laundry consultant and the diaper-changing specialist.

Changing That First Diaper

While you are in the hospital the nurse or midwife will give you a quick lesson on changing your first diaper. These professionals know how to teach first-timers, so listen to them. They are excellent resources. A sister, your mother or mother-in-law can also share diaper-changing knowledge, but hearing the instructions from a professional is easier for a 21st-Century Dad to accept.

The first step in a diaper change is having the tools you need to change the diaper (new diaper, balm, wet wipe, tissues, rubbing alcohol and cotton swabs, and a container for the old diaper). Nowadays, disposable diapers are more popular than cloth diapers. However, you and Mom should discuss this issue prior to Baby's arrival. If you choose disposable diapers, you need to regularly purchase jumbo packs. If you choose cloth diapers, you will most likely consider a diaper service. Either way, your experience will be improved if a changing table equipped with a pad is available. Once the diaper tools are laid out, follow these steps:

1. Lay Baby on his/her back
2. Undo clothes and undergarments and slide them under Baby's back
3. Undo the "sticky" diaper straps (or pins)
4. Lift Baby's legs with one hand and use the diaper to wipe off excess mess
5. Clean and wipe Baby's bottom with your other hand, using a wet wipe or two
6. Slide a new diaper under Baby's bottom so the underside and topside are somewhat equal

First Coach

Hospital nurses know how to teach first-timers, so listen to them.

Within 2 minutes of a new diaper change, Baby will decide to let one rip and fill another diaper. Do you wait a few more minutes and change the diaper, knowing full well that the same thing will occur? Or do you pass Baby to Mom, hoping that she will notice the dirty diaper and change it?

7. Set old diaper out of the way to avoid getting Baby's wandering feet and hands dirty
8. Apply the balm
9. Attach/secure the new diaper
10. Wrap up the old diaper and wet wipe in one bundle
11. Reattach the undergarments and clothes (attaching all snaps)
12. Dispose of the old diaper
13. If the old diaper leaked, remove soiled clothing, pre-treat all stains, scrub and hang to dry

As Baby learns to roll over, remember to keep a hand on him/her while you are reaching for a new diaper or wet wipe because mobile babies move quickly. Also, if Baby is a boy, in Step 3 you may need to place a tissue over Baby's penis to avoid being squirted. One time in the face is usually all the reminder you will need.

Diapers — How Often? — Really!

Trust me on this one. Within 2 minutes of a new diaper change, Baby will decide to let one rip and fill another diaper. Do you wait a few more minutes and change the diaper, knowing full well that the same thing will occur? Or do you pass Baby to Mom, hoping that she will notice the dirty diaper and change it? This decision depends on Mom's location. If she is out shopping, you certainly don't have that option. However, if Mom is in the other room reading or doing something else, you may decide to use the pass technique. I guess the bottom line (pun intended) is that if you were sitting in a diaper filled with mushy yellow liquid, how long would you want to wait for someone to change your diaper? Maybe your kids will remember to change your adult diapers more often when you are 85 if you remembered to change their baby diapers!

In addition to the diaper change, the nurse should have taught you how to care for the umbilical cord stump and how to dress and swaddle Baby. If you were blessed with a baby boy, the nurse also will brief you on proper care for your son's penis, especially if he was circumcised. The next few subsections provide insight on proper care of these topics.

Changing That First Diaper

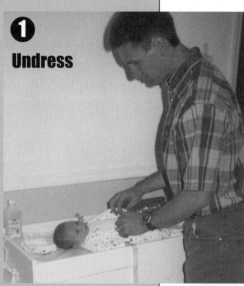

1 Undress

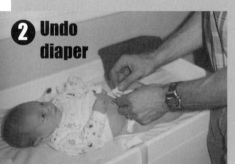

2 Undo diaper

3 Wipe

4 Put on new diaper

Don't worry if it takes longer than you expect. Practice makes perfect!

Umbilical Cord

To lessen the chances of infection and ensure proper development of the navel, it is necessary that you clean the umbilical cord stump during Baby's first weeks of life. This process is simple and requires only a bottle of rubbing alcohol and a cotton swab. All you need to do is dampen the swab with the rubbing alcohol, bend back the umbilical cord stump and carefully moisten the scabby area around the attached stump. Many factors (hot lights, rubbing alcohol treatments, etc.) determine the cord's color and how long the stump

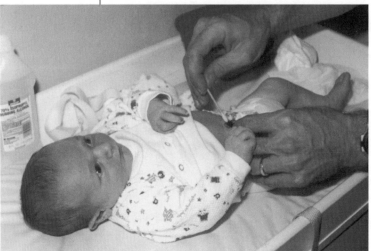

remains attached to Baby's navel. Our first child had her stump for 2 weeks but our second child's stump was attached for 4 weeks. Your job is to keep applying the alcohol until the stump falls off.

The Cord

Your job is to keep applying the alcohol until the stump falls off.

Chapter 4 –
Step-by-Step Plays or How-To's

First Bath

Bathing a newborn is a scary feeling the first few times and requires a detailed game plan to be successful. Follow these preparation steps:

- Place Baby down in a safe place for a few minutes
- Clean the bathing area
- Gather all the bath accessories (bathing sponge and/or tub, baby soap, baby shampoo, drying towel, washcloth, new diaper, new undergarment, skin lotion, balm and a new outfit) Note: If Baby still has the umbilical cord stump, you'll also need rubbing alcohol and a cotton swab.
- Begin to fill up the tub and keep the temperature warm, not hot (if you're unfamiliar with the proper temperature for Baby's bath water, invest in a bath thermometer)

Now that all items are near the bathing area (sink, shower or bath tub) and the water is running, it's time for the bath itself:

- Pick up Baby
- Remove Baby's clothes
- Place Baby in the bath
- Use the washcloth to wring out clean water over Baby (be sure to get Baby's face wet during every bath so Baby won't be afraid of the water)
- Begin to wipe Baby's face without using soap
- Next, clean Baby's head (using baby shampoo)
- Then apply soap to Baby's neck and behind the ears, wash the underarms, arms, legs, feet and back and conclude with the

bottom. (Note: The boy's foreskin of the penis must be carefully pulled back and cleaned)

- Be careful to hold Baby securely when soap is applied because infants are slippery and wriggly
- Rinse Baby with fresh water
- Place Baby on the drying towel
- Dry Baby's bottom, apply diaper balm and lotion and then diaper Baby
- Next, rub lotion on the rest of Baby's body, dress Baby and put Baby in a safe place while you clean the bathing station and hang the towels

Bathing

Even the team's rookie hits the showers

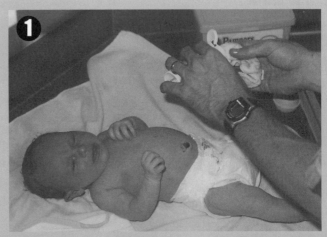

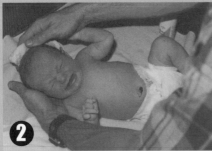

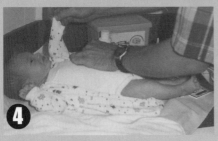

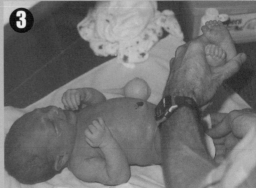

1 **Suds up**
2 **Clean upper body & rinse**
3 **Clean lower body & rinse**
4 **Rediaper and dress**

Swaddling Baby

Swaddling is actually an elementary process that comforts Baby by making him feel snug and secure (like he was inside Mom). All you really need to do is place the swaddling blanket or hooded towel on a flat surface. Then, put Baby's head into the hood of the towel or fold one end of the blanket (approximately 4 inches) inward and place Baby's head on top of the folded side. Next, fold the end closest to the feet up and over Baby's legs to the breastbone. Conclude with the left and/or right flaps wrapping around Baby's torso and tucking under the back. Swaddling in a towel will keep Baby warm if you carry him to his changing table to be dressed. If the blanket is large enough, Baby should remain swaddled for hours. However, if the blanket is too small, even a perfect swaddling job will be unwrapped by a moving Baby.

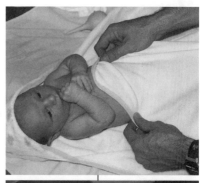

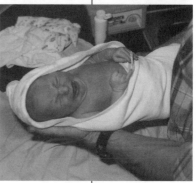

Caring for the Penis (Baby's, not yours)

If your Baby boy was circumcised, you will need to apply petroleum jelly to the diaper after each diaper change for approximately 2 weeks. The jelly reduces friction between the penis and the diaper.

Once the circumcision is healed, your doctor will remind you to regularly pull back the foreskin of the penis to prevent a build-up of skin. This process should be done for <u>at least two years</u> during each bath. The uncircumcised Baby boy's foreskin must also be carefully pulled back and cleaned during each bath.

Spitting Up

There are two things that all Babies do – cry and spit up. First, make sure that Baby is really spitting up – and not choking. Of course, Mom will instruct you to treat the outfit stain and change the sheets immediately after a spit-up. She will also remind you that if you were smart, you would have used a burp cloth to avoid any spit-up mess in the first place.

Avoid Penalties

Mom will instruct you to treat the outfit stain and change the sheets immediately after a spit-up.

WHEN YOUR BABY DOES SPIT UP, IT'S YOUR CALL — WHAT DO YOU DO?

- Do you use a wet wipe or wet cloth to clean up the spill (and then follow protocol, as defined by Mom)?

  or

- Do you wipe everything clean and hope the stain dries before Mom checks on Baby? (Certainly a gamble, but sometimes you just have to take your chances)

Burping Baby

Whether Mom has decided to breast-feed or use formula, Baby must be burped every few minutes when nursing or drinking from a bottle. Here are a few common methods to relieve Baby of gas build-up and, more importantly, to keep you from being the victim of an upchuck.

Game Plan A

- Drape a burp cloth over your shoulder. Then place one hand on Baby's back, and carefully bring Baby to your chest. Tap the middle of Baby's back with a firm open hand, and listen for the burp.

Game Plan B

- Place Baby across your legs, and tap the middle of Baby's back.

Game Plan C

- Hold Baby upright yet tilted slightly, and tap the middle of Baby's back.

When burping Baby or shortly after feeding Baby, be careful if you raise Baby over your head or move her too quickly, otherwise you might be wearing lunch. Mom will be upset if Baby loses lunch and she has to feed again. And – trust me on this one – you'll be upset if the lost lunch is found on you.

Prevent Spitting Up

Be careful if you raise Baby over your head or move too quickly, otherwise you might be wearing lunch.

If Baby cries after a feeding, consider giving the child gas-reducing drops with the active ingredient simethicone. As always, consult with the pediatrician (baby doctor) before using any medicine.

Washing Baby's Clothes

Washing clothes for a newborn is more than adding a few little outfits to your regular laundry. Use a skin-sensitive detergent with the second rinse cycle and no fabric softener. Place the washing machine on the second rinse setting to ensure that all the soap is removed from the clothing (avoid liquid and sheet softeners).

As with new adult clothes, avoid combining new, bright-colored clothes with light-colored clothes. And wash all new items before they are used.

Dressing Baby

When changing Baby's clothes, remember the tag is always in the back — even though the snaps or buttons may be in the front or back of the outfit. Every baby outfit is different, and sooner or later you will dress your child like a geek and Mom will laugh at you.

When you have just changed Baby's clothes and know you will be changing Baby's clothes again in 2 hours, do you take time to snap the three snaps on the undergarment and the 12 snaps on the outfit or do you choose to do most of the snaps? If you are going out in public or people are coming to visit, I advise you to snap all snaps to avoid "the look" from Mom.

Dressing Baby for Weather

Newborns and Babies need to be kept warm and out of the sun and wind. In cold weather, Baby may need a hat, several layers of clothes and an extra blanket. One-piece sleepers also keep Baby comfortable in chilly weather. When the weather is warm or even hot, cover Baby for protection from the sun, and dress Baby in lightweight clothes.

Suiting Up

Remember the tag is always in the back.

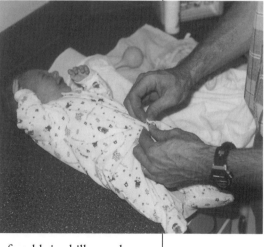

21st-Century Dad

Chapter 5 –
Dad's Typical Questions

How Long Should I Hold Baby?

Babies need to be comforted. And there are many philosophies and ideas on comforting your Child. A warm hug reaffirms to Baby that you provide a safe place for rest. Holding Baby also creates a bond between you and the Child.

If Mom is breast-feeding, she is constantly holding Baby, but your close interaction with Baby is limited to your holding Baby. Again, trust me. Baby grows up quickly, and your opportunities for holding him when he wants to be held is limited. I believe you can never hold Baby too often but you **can** hold Baby too long. Babies need to develop self-confidence and trust in people other than you. If you always allow Baby to fall asleep while being held, you may have difficulty on trips or in unfamiliar places **and** you might create a dependent child.

When holding a newborn, be sure to support Baby's head. For the first 2 months or more, infants do not have much neck strength and must be supported at all times.

Different ways to hold a baby.

21st- Century
Dad

The less time Baby is exposed to the elements of the world and other people's germs during the first few months, the better.

Where Can We Travel Those First Few Weeks?

Absolutely nowhere. You owe it to yourself, Mom and Baby to stay home for about a month. The less time Baby is exposed to the elements of the world and other people's germs during the first few months, the better.

Trips to the grocery store really should be made by Dad, with Mom and Baby remaining at home. If Mom had a C-section or a complicated delivery, she probably won't want to leave home at all. However, in the rare case when Mom needs to get out of the house, she may want to handle some shopping duties. More than likely, you are the designated shopper for a few weeks, and the Family will be home for awhile.

Where Can We Travel After 2 Months?

Anywhere you would like to go (consult with your doctor). Road trips and plane flights are possible but require you — as a 21st-Century Dad — to be patient and willing to plan ahead and allow for the unexpected. When traveling with Baby you have to carry excess baby gear and allocate extra time for crying fits. Leaving the convenience of your home is more than loading up and bringing the necessities with you. It requires that you are serious about the trip. Whether you travel by auto or plane, you will need to transport to your destination the car seat, stroller, diaper bag, port-a-crib, blankets, pacifiers, wet wipes, Baby's toiletries, bibs, burp cloths, baby toys and a bag of clothes complete with extra undergarments and diapers. If Mom is not breast-feeding, formula, bottles and nipples are also a must.

Remember, the items noted above are just for the kid. Anything you might need for yourself is extra. So, Dad, if you golf and usually bring your clubs, maybe not this trip. If Mom usually brings three outfits for each day, she might have to cut to two. Modifying the load is a necessity if you intend to keep your sanity.

The best way to travel is to have friends or family help you load and unload on both ends of the trip. After your first serious trip you will understand why your friends with kids seldom travel anymore or, if they do, why they limit the number of trips per year.

Note: If Baby is less than a year old, for Baby's comfort avoid flying on small commuter planes because pressure changes can hurt Baby's ears more than the controlled pressure changes in larger jets. Also, when taking off or descending, have Baby suck on a bottle or pacifier to help relieve ear pain from pressure changes in any plane.

What About a Pacifier?

Moms and Dads will most likely discuss the use of a pacifier to calm Baby. A pacifier is a device designed to satisfy the natural sucking reflex that all babies have. Although some parents believe a pacifier is an unnecessary crutch, others would pay several thousand dollars for a pacifier if it helped comfort and quiet Baby. Some researchers even suggest that pacifiers help educate the tongue in preparation for speech and help prevent sudden infant death syndrome (SIDS).

If you choose to use a pacifier, keep an eye on the rubber component. Make sure it is replaced before it wears out or rips. Also, keep the pacifier clean and sterile. During the first few weeks you will wash and sterilize the pacifier every time it falls to the floor – and you should. But as time goes on, the rinse-and-wipe-off method often becomes common. I know some Dads use a 5-second rule, meaning that they just wipe the pacifier and give it back to Baby if the pacifier hasn't been on the floor for more than 5 seconds. In public, however, avoid this practice and at least use hot water to clean the rubber portion of the pacifier. A crying child also influences how you handle the dropped pacifier. When it is time to wean Baby from the pacifier, one suggestion is to poke a tiny hole in the end of the rubber portion so Baby is no longer able to enjoy the sucking sensation.

How Soon Can I Show Off Baby?

You will be so proud of your Child that you will want to show off Baby to the entire world. However, it is vital that you allow time for Baby to adjust to new surroundings and increase her ability to fight off illness. When you voluntarily expose a newborn to people, you do so at the risk of letting the Child catch an illness that may require hospitalization. Allowing immediate family and a few close

The 5-Second Rule

When the pacifier hasn't been on the floor for more than 5 seconds, scoop it up, wipe it off and hope the Ref wasn't watching.

friends to see and/or hold Baby during the first few weeks is reasonable. But I suggest you limit other people's contact with Baby as much as possible during the first few weeks of life. Your doctor will confirm this concept.

How Quiet Do We Have to Be for Baby?

Some parents believe you should walk on eggshells when Baby is sleeping, but I suggest that you live your normal life. Baby will adjust to your music and TV habits, the dog barking or the vacuum cleaner if you let Baby fit into your environment. There are certain times (prior to an expected 8 p.m. visit from friends, for example) when you might prefer Baby to sleep. But most days you probably will be fine by just living your normal life.

What If Baby Cries All the Time?

If Baby continues to cry excessively, the problem may be colic. A colicky baby can be a challenge for Dad because no matter what you do to help Baby feel better (namely feed, burp, administer anti-gas drops and change the diaper), Baby continues to cry.

When Baby is crying and you are at your wit's end, keep your cool and remember that crying is Baby's only method for communicating with you. Baby is uncomfortable and needs your assistance. Baby may:

- have a wet/dirty diaper
- be hungry
- be tired
- want to be held
- have gas bubbles in the stomach

Keep The Star Happy

Anti-gas drops may help dissipate gas bubbles in the stomach.

Baby anti-gas drops may help dissipate gas bubbles in the stomach. There are name brands and generic brands (much less expensive) of anti-gas drops, but the active ingredient simethicone is really all you need to look for. In our household, the anti-gas drops proved to be magic for our Babies. As always, consult with your doctor before using over-the-counter medications for Baby.

6

Chapter 6 – Mom's Issues

Communicating with Mom About Child Rearing

Although you and Mom will be ecstatic about Baby's arrival, you and Mom must be on the same page concerning child rearing. Some issues will occur in the infancy stage (i.e., breast feeding, crying), but many child-rearing topics surface when Baby is a toddler. Moms and Dads really should have discussed these issues prior to having Baby, but now the issues are real and must be considered. Here are a few concepts you should discuss:

Review The Playbook

You and Mom must be on the same page concerning child rearing.

- If Mom worked prior to delivery, will she return to work? When?

- If Mom returns to work, how will she handle breast feeding?

- What about breast pump rental/purchase and storage (labeling, bagging and chilling expressed milk)? Does this role change when work schedules change?

- Who will be responsible for making and keeping Baby's medical appointments?

- Who will pack the diaper bag when you leave the house? (Note: I hate that job)

- Where will you store Baby's accessories before birth, during use and after use?

- How will you discipline Baby? Will you use time-out, spanking?

- Will the Child attend private or public school?

- Will you use child care? If so, which type?

- What types of toys and/or learning tools will you purchase? How many? How and where they will be stored?

- Will you begin a college savings fund?

- Will your Child be raised in a religious environment?

- What resources will you provide for the Child (college, computers, etc.)?

- Are there any no-Child zones in the home?

- Who will be responsible for Baby's evening feedings?

- Who will contact the Baby's sitter?

Mom's Bottom Soreness

Expect the first few weeks after Baby's birth to be challenging for all members of the family. However, you must be compassionate as Mom allows her body to heal. Remember, Mom just experienced passing a basketball out of an opening the size of your anus! She will certainly be sore and might be somewhat testy, as well.

During this sensitive period, expect to be yelled at and reminded how easy you have it. During the first few weeks, it's common for Mom to:

- Want to purchase a special perinatal bathing unit (sitz bath) to help the vaginal area heal

- Have to deal with hemorrhoids

- Apply creams, gels or medicated wipes to aid in the healing process

- Complain about using sanitary pads to control excess bleeding

Nurse Mom's Injuries

You must be compassionate as Mom allows her body to heal.

- Dislike bowel movements

- Not even want to think about resuming a sexual relationship

In fact, resuming sexual intimacy will take at least 6 weeks and maybe longer, depending on the delivery. If an episiotomy was performed or a rip occurred during delivery, Mom will require even more healing time.

Cesarean Section

Although cesarean section is common in our society, it is major abdominal surgery and should be treated as such. If your doctor deems that a C-section is necessary, recognize that Mom's recovery will be lengthy and require more effort and understanding on your part. She will not be able to lift or even carry anything heavier than Baby for a few weeks. She will have staples in her belly and extreme soreness once the drugs wear off. The C-section also causes increased inflammation in the abdomen and makes "losing" the tummy very difficult.

Following my wife's C-section, I had to take 2 full weeks off work to help her care for Baby. Additionally, all driving, household chores (cooking, cleaning, laundry) and shopping duties rested upon my shoulders.

Mom's Changing Emotions

Mom will undergo a total emotional transformation during pregnancy and again during the post-partum (or after-delivery) stage. Her emotional fluctuations will catch you off guard and even frustrate you if you don't see them coming. Expect Mom to experience happiness, fear, distress and a myriad of other emotions you probably have never seen before. As Dad, you must be understanding and realize that for 9 months Mom has been creating a human being inside of her. Now, her body must readjust itself and focus on the health of one human again, rather than two.

Mentally, Mom has to deal with the visual side effects of pregnancy (weight gain, varicose veins) as well as the hormonal changes influencing her body. She may cry for no reason, make negative comments toward you and/or Baby and even say she is not fit to be

Anticipate Mom's Emotions

Expect Mom to experience happiness, fear, distress and a myriad of other emotions you probably have never seen before.

a Mom. It is difficult for Mom to see your life relatively unchanged when hers is totally different. She may also begin talking about her maternal instinct to stay at home rather than return to work. If she has long hair, expect her to consider a shorter hairstyle. Regardless of the topic, all you can do is to listen, provide assistance and be supportive — even at 3 in the morning.

Sexual Intimacy

Sex is probably one thing most wanna-be Dads do not consider when they think about having Baby, but they should. If you recall, when you and wanna-be Mom were trying to have Baby, all books and doctors instructed you to observe the ovulation schedule and to increase the frequency of relations. You thought having a baby sounded great! Then the day you find out you and Mom are pregnant, things change. The ultimate goal has been met and frequency, at least for a while, diminishes.

During Pregnancy—Some Moms do not want to have sex during pregnancy because they think it will harm the fetus. Other Moms become extremely horny and desire intimacy. If your wife/partner believes sex will harm Baby, you should realize that your next intimate experience is at least 11 months away. However, if pregnancy enhances Mom's sexual drive, you could be in for a treat.

Enhanced Sex!

Some Moms believe sexual intimacy should be enhanced during pregnancy.

Research suggests that most pregnant Moms can continue a sexual relationship through pregnancy but may need to alter duration and positions as the fetus grows. You and Mom will have to discuss this issue with the doctor and determine what is best for your relationship. I hope, for your sake, that Mom believes sexual intimacy should be enhanced during pregnancy.

After Baby's Arrival—All Dads want to know when they can resume the sexual relationship with Mom after Baby's arrived. IT VARIES. Whether Mom delivers naturally or by C-section, she will need at least 6 to 8 weeks to recover. Moms who have had a difficult delivery and an episiotomy will need even more time. Consult with your doctor, and determine a target date based on your individual circumstances.

Having an idea of when you might be intimate with your wife/partner again is mentally helpful, but realize the target date may change if mental trauma and physical healing are a concern. By nature, Moms will not openly discuss the sex issue among friends, but most Dads will have no problem asking their friends about their individual situations. During my personal discussions (not scientifically valid, I might add), I learned that most Dads resumed a sexual relationship between 3 and 6 months following delivery. If you are fortunate and the healing process is on target, you might be lucky enough to resume a sexual relationship in the second month.

THE Day Finally Arrives—Although you and Mom are excited about resuming an intimate relationship, expect apprehension and a feeling of uneasiness. The doctor will instruct you to use extra lubricant and to be cautious. As a word of advice, Dad, show compassion and remember that Mom has been healing for several months. Otherwise, this might be the last time for a few more months.

The Other Variable—Now that Mom has determined that enough time has passed and she is ready, realize that Baby also dictates when, where and how often you can be intimate. I wrote this section of the book following the interruption of an intimate snuggle I believed would progress but didn't. A newborn cry and a 2-year-old jumping into bed altered the mood.

As a Dad you will have to be patient and find a time when Mom is not too tired and Baby isn't crying. Timing is everything. Yet, until you experience the balancing act for yourself, you won't fully understand the ramifications. Best of luck.

But Wait ...

Baby also dictates when, where and how often you can be intimate.

Typical Questions About Sex—

- Does your sex life change when you have Baby? Yes. The spontaneous response to one another is influenced by Baby. Therefore, pre-planned times may be needed.

- Does the experience feel different? Maybe. The apprehension and pain present during the first few weeks after your sexual relationship resumes will influence duration and positions.

- Can I hurt Mom? Yes, if you are not careful. Compassion and control are critical.

- When can we resume a sexual relationship? Two to three months following delivery, if cleared by the doctor.

Changed Responsibilities Around the House

As a 21st-Century Dad, you will experience several transformations in your daily life. Change of responsibilities is one of them. Not only will you have new child-care assignments such as diaper changing, bathing and removal of spit-up stains on outfits, but Baby's arrival will mandate that you share a greater percentage of the daily household chores than you were used to. If you never did laundry, cooked, washed dishes, watered plants or cleaned the house, there is a very good chance you will experience – firsthand — these tasks after Baby's arrival. Mom will expect you to vacuum or mop the floors, separate the laundry and prepare the meals in addition to taking out the garbage, mowing the grass, cleaning the car and doing whatever traditional chores are common in your household.

If Mom breast-feeds or has a job outside the home, your role will increase even more. In order to create a balance and preserve the sanity of your marriage, you and Mom should discuss the daily chores and responsibilities openly. Determine who will care for the pets, gas up the car, grocery shop and keep up with the mail and bills. More often than not, Dad will be expected to carry a greater share of the load during the first 2 months and when Mom returns to work, if that is part of your agreed-upon plan.

Baby Play Groups (Mom Support)

A weekly gathering of two or more Moms and their Babies is extremely beneficial for Mom, especially during the first year. Baby groups allow Moms to vent their frustrations and share their personal experiences so you, as Dad, will be less likely to hear them. Even if Mom works, encourage her to talk with other new Moms and join a Baby or Mom support group. Her participation in a baby group can be enjoyable for the maturing Child, especially if you do not use day care.

In addition to encouraging Mom to join a Baby or Mom support group, you can support Mom by making occasional unannounced visits home during work hours and by phoning home several times while you're at work. If Mom is caring for little ones, she needs to hear an adult voice and she may need someone to talk to if Baby is constantly crying. When venting is necessary, realize that you are the sounding board and she really doesn't care what kind of day you are having.

Breast vs. Formula Feeding

As a Dad you really don't have much say in this area but you can voice your opinion. Mom is in control of this decision and will determine whether Baby is breast fed, formula fed or fed by a combination of the two. You and Mom need to discuss this topic prior to Baby's arrival, but physical circumstances (i.e., poor milk production, Mom's ailments) may alter the original plan. Encourage Mom to try breast feeding and stick with it. The first month is often the most difficult, and it usually gets much easier thereafter. To be successful Mom has to commit to this method and Dad has to be supportive.

There are several advantages to breast feeding that benefit both Mom and Baby, but there are also some disadvantages.

Advantages:
- Breast milk is available whenever Mom is available
- Breast milk is the best food source you can offer Baby
- Breast milk is free
- You don't have to mix formula or find a blend Baby can digest
- You don't have to sterilize bottles

Mom's Team

Baby groups allow Moms to vent their frustrations and share their personal experiences so you, as Dad, will be less likely to hear them.

- Mom will lose her excess weight more rapidly than if she did not breast-feed
- Mom's boobs will be huge (but please don't touch – they're sensitive)

Disadvantages:
- Breast feeding is fatiguing
- Mom's nipples may be sore in the beginning
- Mom might develop mastitis (an inflammation of the milk ducts), clogged ducts or a thrush infection
- Mom may complain that you don't have to spend hours every day feeding Baby
- Mom will have to use a breast pump on occasion, or possibly daily, to reduce the pressure when she has to be away from the Baby for several hours
- As Dad, you won't be able to feed Baby unless Mom pumps the milk
- Breasts may leak during outings or intimacy

My experience is that most new Moms want to experience breast feeding and do so for at least a few weeks. Some Moms who believe in breast feeding continue for 6 months to 1 year while others extend the time even further. Most pediatricians encourage Moms to breast feed for the first year.

Some Moms decide to quit breast feeding because:
- It may be painful during the first few weeks
- They may be sleep deprived (there could be two night-time feedings in the beginning)
- They get fatigued (producing milk and nursing itself are draining on the body)
- They don't want to pump (especially if they are returning to the workplace, where pumping is not convenient)
- They want Dad to share feeding responsibilities
- Baby hasn't latched on well or stimulated enough milk
- They don't make or don't think they make enough milk
- People tell them Baby will sleep through the night if they're given formula
- They don't feel comfortable nursing in public places or around other people

Feeding Schedules

A **demand** schedule is when you feed Baby when Baby cries, assuming Baby is hungry. A **parent-directed** approach is when you establish a schedule for Baby and stick to it.

Relatives, friends and books written about feeding Baby will share pros and cons about feeding schedules. Ultimately, you and Mom have to determine what is best for your particular situation.

Working Moms almost always have to use the parent-directed approach unless formula is used. Regardless of your method, during the first year expect to spend countless hours feeding Baby. Additionally, expect to spend a significant amount of time cleaning baby bottles and accessories before and after each feeding. If Mom is doing most of the feedings, you will end up doing most of the cleaning and sterilizing. Expect the following cleaning-and-sterilizing game plans:

Formula feeding - After each feeding, the bottle and nipple must be washed in hot water and then boiled (often recommended for the first couple of months) to ensure a sterile environment for the next feeding. In addition to cleaning nipples, bottles and caps, Mom will probably have you washing the bottle holders and pacifiers.

Breast feeding - Anytime Mom expresses milk, it may be your job to clean and sterilize the pumping accessories and/or transfer the milk from a container to the freezer bag for safe keeping. When expressed milk is used, you will

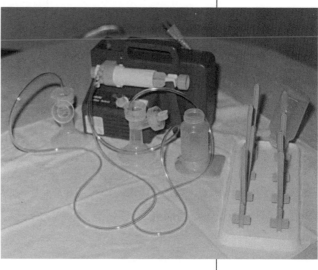

be cleaning bottles, nipples and caps. The breast pump can be purchased or rented, but the accessories need to be purchased to ensure cleanliness.

Bulking Up

During the first year expect to spend countless hours feeding Baby.

59

Warming the frozen milk - To avoid losing nutrients, thaw expressed milk in warm, not hot water. Feed Baby when the milk is lukewarm (do not microwave).

Feeding Baby

As Baby approaches 4 months you, Dad, will have the opportunity to be more involved in the feeding process. Of course, Mom will play a major role, especially if she is breast-feeding. However, now you now have a chance to help feed Baby every day.

The first food most Babies are introduced to is rice cereal. You just mix the powder with a few teaspoons of water or breast milk/formula and shazam! You have mushy rice cereal. This concoction is tasteless and has the consistency of wallpaper paste, yet Babies can digest this food. The challenge is to entice Baby to eat and swallow the rice cereal. Since the nipple is the only oral stimulus Baby has had for several months, the thought of your sticking a spoon in Baby's mouth is foreign so Baby often spits out the cereal. During the first few cereal feedings expect Baby to spit out the cereal and make a face you might make if you bit into an apple and saw half a worm.

Pre-Game Meals

Babies have yet to learn that ice cream and chocolate taste better than peas and squash.

After Baby has the hang of swallowing, you now have the pleasure of introducing real food (translation: very mushy stuff or processed baby food). Although I did not understand at the time why my sister and wife forced me to feed Baby vegetables first, I now do. Babies have yet to learn that ice cream and chocolate taste better than peas and squash. So, if you introduce Baby to foods they will most certainly like, you may have a difficult time making them eat foods that are good for them. I encourage you to use this strategy because when Baby is 1 year old and eats everything, your friends will be jealous.

When you introduce new foods to Baby, remember to introduce only one food every few days. Because you have no idea if Baby is allergic to certain foods, avoid mixing foods so it'll be easier to determine the source of an allergic reaction and/or rash. If Baby does react to a certain food, write down the food and then talk with your pediatrician at the next office visit.

Although I am glad my child was exposed to healthy food early on, and now has fairly good eating habits, I have to admit that when Mom wasn't around my little girl had some ice cream, whipped cream, soft drinks and a few other tasty treats that Dads know Babies must have. The first time my Baby had a fast-food french fry and soft drink, I felt like I was a kid sneaking a cookie. Dad, you have a responsibility to be the "good Parent" every now and then – an ice cream cone or a trip to a fast-food chain will bring a smile to Baby's face. (But, don't tell Mom.)

Doctor (Pediatrician)

Some pediatricians will encourage you to schedule well-baby appointments for shots and regular check-ups either early in the morning or just after lunch, when the waiting room is clean and disinfected, or at least less crowded. Using this strategy may help Baby avoid catching illnesses from other sick kids in the waiting room. As a Dad, get to know the pediatrician and be familiar with Baby's immunization schedule and medical history. Mom generally takes on this responsibility. However, if she is out of town, at work or ill herself and Baby appears sick, it's your responsibility to visit the doctor (that means knowing where the office is), administer medicine and nurse Baby. Nowadays, children should have the entire series of immunizations before they start school. Be sure to keep accurate medical records for your Child.

Social Circles

Soon after you find out you are pregnant, your social circles will gradually be adjusted. Your circle of single friends and friends without children are not comfortable discussing children nor do they care to hear about your pregnancy. On the other hand, friends with children enjoy hearing your story because it is a platform for them to share theirs.

On occasion, you and Mom may enjoy a Saturday night dinner and a movie or socializing with two or three couples but, on average, the evening will be modified into a dinner or a movie and then home to bed. At first, this change might be difficult for some

New Friends

Your social circles will gradually be adjusted.

couples, but over time you will realize that the Family is now your priority and missing a late-evening adventure is just fine.

Shower and Post-Birth Gifts

If you are fortunate to have thoughtful friends and family members, you will undoubtedly receive several gifts celebrating Baby's arrival. At first you will feel funny accepting gifts from work associates, relatives you haven't seen in years and your parents' friends. But once you realize the gifts are a blessing, you will appreciate their thoughtfulness and know you will return the favor when others have their first Baby.

Similar to a bridal registry, a baby registry helps your friends buy what you really need. Although it might seem improper or "forward" to register for specific baby gifts, through a registry you'll increase the likelihood that you'll receive gifts you really need rather than a surplus of undergarments, sleepers and stuffed animals. You and Mom should tour two or three department or baby stores and make logical purchasing decisions that fit your home's motif.

Whether gifts roll in before, during or after a baby shower, you must write down who gives you what and be sure to send a thank-you card acknowledging your gratitude. In most cases, Mom assumes the responsibility of purchasing, addressing and writing brief notes to thank friends and family members. To speed up the process and ensure that all gift bearers are thanked within 1 week, you may opt to write the thank-you notes to your family members and close friends. Although I am not often found doing this chore, it really should be shared by both Parents.

Birth Announcements

When Baby finally arrives after 9 long months, you will be on top of the world and want to share your joy with your friends and family members. You and Mom will have to decide whether you will purchase custom-made birth announcements, make them on your computer or buy them from a full-service store. Whatever you decide, you have to determine who is to receive an announcement, whether or not you will send a picture and, if so, which picture. Again, discuss who will take the time to address and

Line-Up Card

A baby registry helps your friends buy what you really need.

distribute the birth announcements. Make sure you and Mom are on the same page when you are preparing the announcements.

When our first Child arrived, my wife and I were so proud and thought everyone should have a picture of our beautiful newborn. Let's face it, all newborns are less than attractive to everyone in the world except the Parents and Grandparents. Friends and family members will ask you for a picture and certainly look at it. But as you reflect upon Baby's 2-hours-old picture and compare it to the 3-month picture, you will realize that the Baby you were so proud to show off was not movie star material. My advice is to send the birth announcement right away and wait 3 or 4 months to send a picture.

Toys for Dad

Whatever hobbies you had before Baby arrives will certainly take a back seat to the new Child. Dads have to realize that for a period of at least 2 to 3 years motorcycles, snowmobiles, boats, motor homes, guns, balls, bats, golf clubs and racquets must be sold or given more rest for a while.

If you have hobbies that allow you to bring Baby with you (i.e., golf range, tennis court), you may be able to modify your participation and continue to enjoy them. I suggest you talk to Mom and schedule one day each month when she will visit with her friends or relatives while you can spend the entire day enjoying your pastime. There is a catch, of course. You should return the favor for Mom each month. Furthermore, you have to keep up with the Honey-do list at least 3 days preceding your day out. If you fail to complete your Honey-do's, your planned outing will not take place without severe repercussions. The popularity of cell phones has increased the likelihood that Dad will be granted his day out.

Free Time

Free time is essential for both Mom and Dad and should be carefully planned into the day's and week's activities. If you have to hire a sitter or use friends or a relative, be sure to schedule a few hours of free time each week. Mom and Dad should also have time together, away from Baby, to allow their relationship to grow. A

Play Baby First

Hobbies you had before Baby arrives will certainly take a back seat to the new Child.

Game Scheduling

With proper planning and Mom's endorsement, a leisure experience confined to one morning or one afternoon a week can be realistic.

healthy mental attitude for Mom and Dad translates into a healthy relationship between Parents and Baby. A modification of pre-Baby activities is necessary. However, total denial of activities that were important to Mom and Dad may result in frustration and arguments.

In my opinion, you'll be a better Dad if you periodically allow yourself free time to engage in the leisure activities you enjoy. Stopping at the bar on the way home from work, hanging out with the guys every Wednesday night or going fishing for the weekend are probably out of the question. However, with proper planning and Mom's endorsement, a leisure experience confined to one morning or one afternoon a week can be realistic. If you hunt, fish, golf or enjoy working on your car for a few hours, coordinate a Child-sharing schedule with Mom. To improve your chances of securing a 4-hour outing, offer Mom a similar outing to visit with friends, shop, exercise, get her hair done or do whatever she enjoys. Let Mom enjoy the experience first so she will be more likely to reciprocate. When she returns from the outing, no matter how difficult Baby has been, say, "Honey, the day was great. The baby and I became closer and we read books, watched sports and finished the laundry. Did you have fun with your friends? Let me see what you bought!"

If you jog, consider buying a jogger designed for Babies and hit the road whenever the weather cooperates. This two- or three-hundred-dollar investment provides you the freedom to exercise with Baby, enjoy the fresh air and give Mom a break from Baby duty. If you play in a softball or volleyball league, Mom and Baby can attend games with you. However, to make this work, you are responsible for pre-game chores (Translation: make the meal, change the diaper, dress Baby, load the stroller, bring the bottle and completely equipped diaper bag and buckle Baby in the car seat.) When you get home, take your shower immediately and then bathe Baby and begin your evening routine. Each and every time Mom affords you free time, go overboard to let her know you appreciate her support. Otherwise, your next outing may be way down the road.

An important aspect of free time is talking with Mom after Baby goes to bed. You will be inundated with Child-care responsibilities and may forget to talk with her. Make time to visit casually without a preconceived agenda.

If you are preparing for a baptism or first birthday, significant planning is necessary to adequately handle your visitors. If you enjoy having friends over for a movie or cards in your free time, remember that plan must include children or you must find a sitter.

Work Schedules

Work is an important real-life item that will affect your relationship when Baby arrives. You and Mom have to determine how your Family will balance work schedules and baby responsibilities on a daily, monthly and annual basis. Typical questions many Dads and Moms discuss are:

- Will Mom continue to work when the baby arrives (if she does now)? While pregnant, some Moms have every intention of returning to work. But when Baby arrives and the maternal instinct kicks in, they prefer to stay home.

- If Mom intends to return to work, at what point will she return to work? Will she work part or full time?

- Can the Family make it on one salary? In a world where women have become major contributors to a family's financial base, you may need to decide if Mom will work while you stay at home (I mean, this **is** the 21st Century, Dad). Previous generations could make ends meet on one salary. Your Family may be able to make due with some sacrifices, but most families require two incomes to live comfortably in today's world.

If at all possible I encourage you to request 2 weeks off when Baby arrives and then do what you have to do at work to avoid problems with your boss. Mom will need your help, and you won't be very productive at work anyway. Once you resume a "normal" work schedule, know where you stand when you come home from work. Does Mom bail and leave you with Baby? Do you work together and share responsibilities? Do you say, "Honey, I'm home, see you in a few hours after my golf game"?

First Week Home

Mom will need your help, and you won't be very productive at work anyway.

21st-Century Dad

Some Moms will have Dads care for other children, care for the animals, handle yard and auto maintenance and even ask them to cook the evening meal. Other Moms will hand Baby over and head to the mall. KNOW where you stand, and ask Mom how she feels about your role once you come home from work.

Chapter 7 –
Other People's Influence on Baby

Relatives

This section could probably be an entire book for many families. As a Dad, you and Mom need to be on the same page when it comes to relatives and Baby.

Initially, you need to address how much your mother-in-law should help out, determine whether or not she will live with you and, if so, how long? In-laws can be great for the Family or cause internal feuding between you and Mom. Take time to discuss the in-laws and their philosophy on child rearing before you find yourself in a situation where you and the in-laws disagree. In-laws and other family members can serve as excellent resources. But keep in mind that now you are the Dad and that entitles you to use the statement "Under my roof you will play by my rules."

What if relatives do not agree with your child-rearing methods? Listen to their suggestions and consider their methods. But, when push comes to shove, lay down the law, ask for their support and endorsement, and implement the philosophy you and Mom have chosen. Hopefully, they will respect your status as a Dad even if your philosophy differs from theirs.

Friends' Babies and Comparing

It is natural to want to compare Baby with other kids of similar age for several reasons. Be proud of Baby's accomplishments but avoid getting frustrated because your friends' Babies crawl or walk before your Baby does. If you believe Baby is not on target concerning common stages of growth and development, ask your doctor.

In-laws

Take time to discuss the in-laws and their philosophy on child rearing before you find yourself in a situation where you and the in-laws disagree.

Sometimes when you compare Baby's progress with your friends' Babies, you will be pleasantly surprised. Other times you will be disappointed. I can recall feeling disappointed because my little girl didn't walk until 13 months when all of her baby-group friends were walking. Now she runs as well as, or better than, her friends. On the other hand, I also remember bragging about her sleeping through the night after 9 weeks when our friends' kids didn't sleep through the night until 1 year.

In casual conversation show an interest in the development of your friends' or family's children but always be proud of your Baby's progress and let nature take its course. Avoid pushing Baby. Rearing kids requires a committed effort on your part as Dad, but realize that progress through several developmental stages occurs differently for every Baby.

Baby's Looks

Part of the excitement of having Baby is knowing that somehow, someway, your genes and chromosomes have contributed to Baby's looks. Whether they come out 6 pounds or 10, dark-haired or light-haired, end up with brown eyes or blue eyes, you will undoubtedly find a personal characteristic or family trait resembling your side of the family. How important is this? Not very, but it's fun to talk about Baby, knowing full well that no matter how Baby looks physically, Dad will love Baby more than the sun, the moon and the stars.

Match-Ups

Show an interest in the development of your friends' or family's children but always be proud of your Baby's progress and let nature take its course.

Chapter 8 — Common Firsts

You can look forward to several common "first" experiences in the upcoming years. Some are rewarding and require being captured on film and video. Others are disheartening and make you wish they had never occurred.

My advice to you is to **never** say you saw Baby succeed at a "benchmark task" when Mom was out of the house. Even if you observe the first smile, let Mom be the one to tell **you** she saw it first. On the other hand, if a near-tragic situation occurs, share the experience with Mom so she might avoid a similar experience.

Here are a few common "first" experiences you might observe as a Dad and Baby's approximate age when they might occur:

Experience	When
Smile at your face	2 months
Roll over	4 months
Sit up	6 months
Stand with support	7 months
Crawl	8 months
Step with support	9 months
Say a word	11 months
Walk	12 months
Potty success	18 months and up
Illness	Anytime
Injury	Anytime
Time when you misplace the child	Anytime
Fall from a height	Anytime
Object in the nose or ears	18 months and up

You Saw It First?

Never say you saw Baby succeed at a "benchmark task" when Mom was out of the house.

First Birthday/Religious Occasion

During the first year you and Mom will discuss a few celebrations in Baby's life. Some Parents will discuss christening while others will wait until the first birthday. Regardless of when you plan the first major event, you and Mom need to discuss just how elaborate the function will be and ask these questions:

- When will it be?
- What is the budget?
- Who will be invited?
- Will the food be home-prepared or catered?
- Who will write and send the invitations?

Several questions must be discussed at length because hosting a major party when you have to deal with the uncertainty of a new Baby is a challenge. Take time to talk with Mom in advance.

First Professional Photo

Most Parents have Baby's first picture taken when Baby is about 3 months old. However, this decision is totally up to the Parents. Three months is common because, at this age, most Babies can smile on cue and have "filled out" somewhat. But, again, this is a personal choice.

When you do decide to have Baby's picture taken by a professional, this "first" experience is one you will not forget. If Baby is an angel and appears to love the photo shoot, you will boast to your friends about how easy and enjoyable the outing was. However, if Baby spits up on the outfit just before the picture, falls asleep or screams during the poses, your perception of the experience will be skewed.

To increase your chances of having a positive photo experience, make an appointment with a reputable photographer and arrange your feeding schedule so Baby will be alert just prior to the appointment. In case of a mishap, bring alternate clothing. To reduce Baby's anxiety, both Dad and Mom should attend the photo shoot, even if a Family portrait is not going to be taken. However, a professional Family photo is nice to have at various stages of development. Once the pictures are taken, you and Mom will have to

Team Picture

To increase your chances of having a positive photo experience, make an appointment with a reputable photographer and arrange your feeding schedule so Baby will be alert just prior to the appointment.

decide which pictures to choose, what size and how many. If you are like most Dads, you will express your opinion and then be overruled by Mom. Most of us guys don't really care. We just want to get home.

Some photographers will display the pictures on the computer and then encourage you to purchase holiday and specialty cards or specialty frames. To avoid being an impulsive consumer, talk with Mom about the packages **before** the photo shoot. Otherwise, you may be enticed to purchase unnecessary pictures.

First Time Alone with Baby

The first time Mom entrusts you to care for Baby is an adventure. You will be secretly terrified, want to know how Mom can be reached and hope that nothing goes wrong while she is gone. An hour or two isn't much of a challenge. But 4 to 6 hours of full-time Baby duty will test your skills and possibly your patience.

Hopefully, you will know where to find all of Baby's accessories, but if you don't, somehow you'll be sure to find them. I can remember really enjoying my first solo experience with my daughter. She and I read books, ate a snack and then snuggled on the couch and watched football together. Mom left us directions to eat every 3 hours and we did. I also had to change a few wet and dirty diapers. Otherwise, Baby slept most of the time.

Although the first experience was fine, other occasions were not as easy. I also remember Baby fussing and crying the entire time Mom was gone. I tried rocking, walking, talking and even different kinds of music, but nothing worked. Then, when Mom came home all I heard was how tough her day was. Dad, listen and learn from my experience. No matter how difficult your day with Baby might be, when you are babysitting and Mom is out, expect to receive no sympathy — even if you have a miserable experience. Mom's attitude will most likely be that she deals with these problems every day, so you should too. Just accept it and move on. It's not worth arguing about.

Home Alone

4 to 6 hours of full-time Baby duty will test your skills and possibly your patience.

First Restaurant Experience

To improve your chances of having an enjoyable dinner with Mom and Baby, you must plan ahead. First, consider a restaurant where the wait is minimal (use this same strategy with toddlers, too), the service is fast and the crowds/atmosphere are acceptable for Baby. Smoke-filled and loud establishments or fine dining restaurants are not really the place to go for the first few outings. Typically, an early dinner is best because the crowds are sparse and the service is focused on you rather than a dozen other tables.

Second, attempt to feed Baby just before you leave for the restaurant. Hopefully, a full belly will minimize crying and help Baby fall asleep.

Third, use the carrier car seat and place it **securely** in the corner on the table or chair and against a wall, out of traffic. Your Baby is precious, but you can't expect busy servers to watch out for Baby as you do in your own home. Steer clear of aisleways and areas where large trays are being carried.

Finally, I recommend that you resume the eating-out plan you had before Baby arrived. If you ate out once each week, continue to do so. Baby should complement your life, not control it. If you plan effectively, you should be able to enjoy a lunch or dinner out on the town.

Eating Out

You can't expect busy servers to watch out for Baby as you do in your own home.

First Tooth

Another benchmark for Babies is the first tooth. Anytime beyond 3 months you can expect to see Baby drooling, biting his hands or other objects and being irritable. Cutting teeth can be painful for Babies and may also influence their desire to eat. So, when Baby is around 5 to 8 months old, expect to see new teeth and some behavior changes. If Mom is breast-feeding, she will certainly let you know when Baby's first tooth arrives. (The tongue usually protects Mom from the new bottom teeth, but she may still seek your sympathy.) To help Baby out, purchase numbing gel – which works for only a few minutes, I might add — and a few chewing toys that are made to be chilled.

First Illness or Cut

The first time your precious Baby appears ill and lethargic, you will feel helpless. Baby will most likely feel warm to the touch, may cry and may act much differently than normal. If Baby is less than 1 month old, call the doctor immediately. Consult with your doctor and determine how you should handle this "first" illness.

If Baby falls and is bleeding, expect to freak out. It is normal for first-time Dads to be over-cautious. The first ear infection, the first cut, the first bruise — all hurt you more than they hurt Baby, so hang in there and do your best. You and Mom need to work as a team when Baby is ill or injured. Avoid blaming Mom for the accident, even if you believe she may have contributed to the outcome.

Is Baby Okay?

It is normal for first-time Dads to be over-cautious.

21st-
Century
Dad

9

Chapter 9 —
Financial Issues

Having Baby definitely has an impact on the Family budget. You and Mom will have to make decisions based on personal finances as well as the impact the item/service has on Baby. The following issues are common in most households.

Child Care

Whether you and Mom work or have determined that only one will work outside of the home, the issue of child care will arise. If child care is the option, you'll have several decisions to make.

First, determine whether or not Baby's care provider will come to your house, whether you will take Baby to the caretaker's house or if you will use a chain child-care center. Even if Mom does not work outside the home, the issue of child care will be discussed because she may want time for herself and need a few hours each week to handle personal issues. As Baby approaches toddler age, child care may be even more important to you and Mom because Baby could benefit from social interaction with other children.

Used and Recycled Clothes

Another potentially sensitive financial issue between Moms and Dads is how they will dress Baby. Some families clothe their Babies by finding deals at garage sales. Others shop only at elite department stores. Since newborns seem to grow out of their clothes every few weeks, you have to ask yourself how much you really want to spend on their outfits. Babies certainly cannot wear out clothing at this age, but they can easily ruin clothes (remember those untreated stains?). Most Families and some friends share newborn and baby

New Uniforms?

Since newborns seem to grow out of their clothes every few weeks, you have to ask yourself how much you really want to spend on their outfits.

clothes among themselves, but you and Mom need to decide what is best for your situation.

Baby Advertisements

As new Parents you and Mom will be inundated with baby-care advertisements every day. Some advertisers will sell you magazines while others will offer you discounted or free baby items, just to attract your business. You and Mom will have to decide if purchasing baby-care magazines and joining baby clubs is best for you, but I highly encourage you to use the free coupons. Since you are most likely going to purchase specific baby items anyway, you might as well take advantage of coupons that offer free or reduced-price merchandise.

Sitters

Whether or not Mom works outside the home, the issue of sitters for Baby will come up. Ideally, relatives and close friends are the best choice because you can trust them. But, remember, they may not always be available when you need them. Many new Parents have three or four possible sitters to call in a pinch. What do you look for in a sitter? Consider the following:

- Make sure the sitter has experience with infants
- Look for sitters who are recommended by someone you trust
- Ask sitters what current certifications they have (CPR, first aid, etc.)
- Ask sitters how they would handle particular situations (fire, bumping Baby's head, etc.)
- Discuss pay in advance

Before you leave Baby with a sitter, provide the sitter with a tentative schedule of your outing and a legitimate way to reach you (cell phone, beeper, phone number, etc.). Take time to show the sitter where all baby-care items are located and how you want Baby cared for. To avoid unnecessary accidents, it is probably best to give Baby a bath before you leave.

How many times should you call home when you are out? Some parents call every 20 minutes. Others never call at all. Talk with Mom and then do what you both believe is right. With our first child, my wife and I always called every 2 hours or less when she was very small.

Child Activities

My guess is that most Parents do not discuss toddler issues until Baby becomes a toddler. However, if Mom and Dad are on the same page concerning issues that require a chunk of the Family budget, a discussion could prevent an argument. You and Mom might want to discuss whether your Child will be enrolled in:

- Child development programs or Montessori school
- Karate classes
- Crafts and art classes
- Music classes
- Church groups
- Gymnastics

If you do choose to enroll your Child in extracurricular activities, discuss with Mom the issues of time, number of sessions per week and transportation. To avoid unnecessary arguments with Mom, develop a plan to address these issues. Sometimes work-related issues are out of your hands and will make you too late for Baby's class. Recognize that this situation is normal, and you need to communicate with Mom. From what I have heard from friends, being a taxi for toddlers is much easier than transporting older children and teenagers.

Off-Season Activities?

To avoid unnecessary arguments with Mom, develop a plan to address your child's activities.

21st-
Century
Dad

10

Chapter 10 —
Miscellaneous Issues

Reading to Baby

Some Dads assume that reading to their Babies is Mom's job. Avoid this belief and enjoy reading with your child. If children learn that reading is cool for Dad — the fun Parent — they may be more interested in reading as they grow. Dad has the ability to use the deep voice and make the big, bad wolf really "big and bad" and the papa bear from The Three Bears a paternal figure they can relate to. Enjoy reading with your Baby from day one, and you will help develop a special bond and personal relationship that will last a lifetime.

Multiple Kids (Twins, etc.)

As noted previously, this book was written to deal with one Baby. But, in today's society, where twins and multiple births are frequent, you may find yourself dealing with two or more Babies. I have several friends with twins and have listened to their stories of late-evening feedings, trips to the doctor, visiting friends and doubling everything — multiple car seats, double the diapers and two kids crying at once. I tip my hat to them for keeping their sanity and moving forward. If you find yourself dealing with multiple births, consider charts, checklists and bulk purchases, but be sure to give as much time to each Child as you can.

Baby's Safety

One way of keeping Baby safe is to reduce the chance of illness by keeping Baby away from large crowds and sick people. Use common sense and avoid situations that could harm Baby. Other ways

Reading Is Cool

If children learn that reading is cool for Dad — the fun Parent — they may be more interested in reading as they grow.

of keeping Baby safe are straightforward. As a 21st-Century Dad, review them and discuss them with Mom:

- Never place Baby's portable carrier on the table or counter top unattended
- Never leave Baby in a vehicle, even for a minute
- Never leave Baby in a stroller
- Never leave Baby unattended, especially if other kids and/or flying objects (as in a park) are in the vicinity
- Never leave Baby unattended in the bathtub
- Never leave Baby around any pet — you can't anticipate how the pets **or** Baby might respond

Baby-Proofing Your House

Several safety items are on the market to help you and Mom prevent accidents in your home. Most safety items are not really an issue until Baby is able to crawl and walk. However, pre-planning and effective Baby-proofing during infancy may give you a feeling of preparedness. The following items are manufactured by several companies and can be purchased in most department and baby stores. Dads usually install most of these Baby-proofing items at home:

- Electrical outlet covers
- Cabinet locks (especially where poison and/or chemicals are present)
- Baby-proof door handles
- Spout protector for the bathtub

In addition, Dads will want to:
- Relocate breakable items from lower shelves to upper shelves
- Cut the cords on all window blinds (avoid Baby being strangled by a looped cord)
- Install additional eyehook locks on exterior doors
- Relocate items that can harm Baby (pencils, kitchen utensils)
- Relocate candles and valuable breakables
- Install corner protectors
- Install gates (stairs and decks)
- Install second-story window locks

The Safety

Pre-planning and effective Baby-proofing during infancy may give you a feeling of preparedness.

Baby-proofing

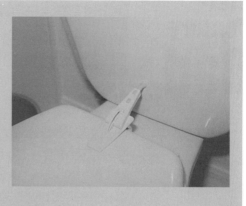

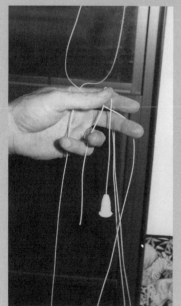

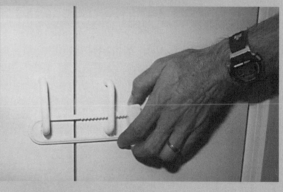

In a matter of minutes, you can help protect your baby.

Eating and Accessories

Eating accessories are not really an issue for the first few months, but when the time comes (at about 4 to 6 months), Dads must know what to do.

The first time you are put in charge of feeding cereal to Baby, you won't know how much to feed Baby, how to wipe excess food from Baby's face or how fast to feed Baby. Most likely, you will hold and feed Baby at the same time. After you mix the cereal and water, set up the feeding station (burp cloth, napkin, wet wipe and tray table), and put a bib on Baby. These tools will help you improve the dining experience as Baby grows:

- Non-spill cups
- Plastic forks and plates
- Portable high chair
- Traditional high chair or conversion high chair (can be used as a table in years to come)
- Bibs
- Snack cup
- Cup with sliding top

A toddler's place-setting options

Buying New Shoes

Avoid being embarrassed by shoe clerks when they tell you Baby's shoes are two sizes too small. The days of wrapping feet are ancient and should not involve your child. As you can surmise, I have had one experience I would have rather not had. Learn from my ignorance and avoid being embarrassed by a shoe salesperson.

Baby Book

Although a baby book is not essential in child rearing, it can serve as a helpful resource for Parents and relatives. The book is an excellent place to record immunizations, physical accomplishments and Baby's "firsts." Although you need to keep up with a baby book to efficiently document benchmarks, I have to say I have never completed an entry in either of my children's baby books. Do I know how to find the book? I think so, but it may take a while.

Planning Extra Time

After Baby arrives, you'll need to plan more effectively to accomplish the same tasks you did before. Going out to dinner with Mom and Baby is more than jumping in the car and heading to the restaurant. With the Baby factor, you have to pack the diaper bag, consider the feeding schedule and evaluate the type of restaurant. As a new Dad, you certainly want to avoid being embarrassed by a screaming Baby in an exclusive establishment. Certain restaurants do cater to families and children and are more receptive to crying Babies and lively toddlers. To avoid waiting for a table in restaurants that don't take reservations, go out to eat during the week rather than the weekend and as early as possible. And, when Baby starts eating table foods, dine in establishments that quickly serve bread, chips, crackers or other appetizers and snacks to occupy your fidgety Child.

When you are planning to be some place at a particular time (church, doctor's appointments, etc.), allow additional time (15 to 20 minutes) if you need to be punctual. Just getting out of your house with the diaper bag and an extra blanket, and loading the baby in the car seat, takes additional time. Furthermore, make time for the unexpected — the unexpected bowel movement that leaks through the outfit or the spit-up that soils Baby's shirt. When you

Extra Innings

You'll need to plan more effectively to accomplish the same tasks you did before.

Keep an extra shirt for yourself in the vehicle.

are in a hurry, expect Baby to spit up on your clean shirt just as you're walking out the door. Keep your patience, and realize that Babies will not conform to your schedule. Be flexible and plan ahead. A word to the wise — keep an extra shirt for yourself in the vehicle and keep a complete change of clothes for Baby in the diaper bag at all times.

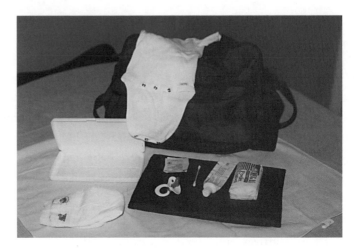

Chapter 11 — Toddlers

Once Baby is walking and moving freely, you have several new-Dad issues to address. Because there is no particular science to child rearing — especially toddlers — I will note only a few specific behaviors you and Mom can expect to observe when your little one approaches 2 years. Toddlers:

Game Rules

There is no particular science to child rearing — especially toddlers.

- Use the word "no," repeatedly
- Might climb and explore — so, Baby-proof your home and establish boundaries for Baby
- Will test your patience in several ways – again, the word NO will be used
- Will refuse to eat and will throw food, eating utensils and cups on the floor – in other words, expect to clean up the same mess over and over
- May color on the walls or step out of a diaper in the middle of the room
- Will want a say in their clothes selection for the day
- Will be picky about types of food to eat
- Will develop a personality of their own — remember, at times the personality may or may not be the personality you might hope for
- Will throw temper tantrums at the most inopportune times – they will arch their backs, kick and scream, and may even hit you during a tantrum
- May be aggressive toward the Family, pets or other children
- May throw a fit if you forget to bring a drink, snack or toy when you are away from home
- May experience night-time terrors — this means they may be unable to sleep in their own beds and will want to sleep with Mom and Dad

Striking Deals

You need to decide when to overrule the Child's behavior. You just can't say NO every time the toddler does something wrong – you might be saying NO all the time! So, as the Dad, you must choose your battles.

Safety concerns — such as fire, electrical sockets, the stove, leaving the house, playing with unsafe items and refusing to hold hands in parking lots and when crossing streets — are an absolute NO in our Family. However, we try to avoid creating unnecessary tantrums over selection of the day's outfit. We try to provide choices for the Child and let her know she can select either this outfit or that one.

Go ahead, strike deals with your toddler. Although I said I would never strike a deal with a 2-year-old, I have and probably will again. If you are in the middle of grocery shopping and your child begins to throw a fit, a quick piece of candy, a cookie or a snack can save the day.

Teach your toddler about choices and consequences. Mom and I believe the sooner a child learns that every choice results in a plus or minus consequence, the better. Although you can't reason with a 2-year-old, you can help them understand scenarios if you present them effectively. You and Mom should discuss the discipline approach you intend to use.

Preserving Memories

Cameras and video recorders are an excellent way to preserve the memories with Baby, but the best way to create a memory is to be there. Dad, you can never re-create a once-in-a-lifetime memory. So, if at all possible, take time in every day to play with Baby, teach your toddler and give your Child the best gift you have – your time.

Mid-Game Snack

If you are in the middle of grocery shopping and your child begins to throw a fit, a quick piece of candy, a cookie or a snack can save the day.

A Day in the Life of the Author

The author (Dad), a 37-year-old, full-time university administrator, has been a Dad for almost 3 years. His wife (Mom), a 32-year-old, full-time university instructor, is dedicated to breastfeeding their children through age 1. The eldest child is a girl (Jana) with an intense desire to ask questions and little desire to potty train. Their 2-month-old boy (Chase) must eat every 3 hours and, until he was 10 weeks old, did not believe that the hours of 2 a.m. and 4 a.m. are times when most people prefer to sleep. With the assistance of grandparents, Mom and Dad have been able to retain full-time employment and maintain a sincere commitment to the Family. The following narration represents a typical 24-hour period in the household.

Monday morning

6:00 a.m. — The day begins with the sound of the alarm.

Mom: "Honey, could you get the baby?"

Dad: "I'm sooooo tired, do we have to go to work today?"

Mom: "Come on Honey, please, we have to get going."

Dad: "OK. — Chase, let's go, buddy, time to see Mom."

Mom: "Honey, did you remember to get the burp cloth?"

Dad: "It's right here."

Mom: "Could you also get me a drink of water?"

Dad: "Sure! What do you want for breakfast?"

Mom: "How about cereal and fruit."

Dad: "We had that yesterday!"

Mom: "If you want something else, you go to the store tonight. I have been busy at work, my boobs hurt and I'm shot."

Dad: "Cereal and fruit are fine. Let me get Jana up."

6:15 a.m.

Dad: "Jana, time to get up. Come on, sleepy head, let's go."

Child: "I don't want to get up, Daddy."

Dad: "That's OK. We're going to get up anyway because Nanny is coming to pick you up in an hour. Jana, how's your diaper?"

Child: "Doin' good!"

Dad: "Let's try the potty."

Child: "I don't want to."

Dad: "Big girls use the potty. Your friend McKenzie uses the potty."

Child: "I use the diaper."

Dad: "OK, little girl, let's change your diaper and have breakfast."

Child: "Daddy, hold me."

Dad: "Come on, let's eat."

Child: "I want my milk."

Mom: "Honey, did you remember to take out the garbage?"

Dad: "Yes, did it last night."

Child: "Daddy, I want my milk."

Dad: "Let's put you in your high chair, and I'll make cereal for you and Mommy."

Child: "OK, Daddy."

Mom: "Honey, I'm done feeding and burping the baby. Could you change him?"

Dad: "Be right there."

6:30 a.m.

Mom: "Honey, be sure to clean him really well and use ointment because he has diaper rash."

Dad: "All right."

Mom: "I'm going to take a shower."

Dad: "Chase, you really had to go! Let's change you and we'll go see your big sister."

Child: "Daddy, I want more milk."

Dad: "Just a minute, Jana. I have to finish changing Chase's diaper. Be right there."

Child: "Daddy, I want juice."

Dad: "Jana, be patient and I will get you some, but first I have to put Chase in his swing and get your diaper bag ready for Nanny."

Child: "Daddy, I want juice right now!"

Dad: "Here you go, angel. Chase, please don't cry now. Mom, are you almost done? I have to go to work, too!"

Mom: "I'll be done in a few minutes. Did you feed and take out the dog?"

Dad: "Not ye-e-e-et, but I will."

<hr>

6:45 a.m.

Mom: **"Remember to pick up the pictures on the way home."**

Dad: "OK. What are we having for dinner tonight?"

Mom: **"I don't care. Whatever you want."**

Dad: "I have to shave and get going because I have an 8 o'clock meeting. Jana is still in the high chair, and Chase is in the swing."

Mom: **"OK! What did you make for breakfast?"**

Dad: "Just cereal and fruit."

Mom: **"Thank you, Honey."**

<hr>

7:00 a.m.

Dad: "Let's finish our breakfast, Jana. I have to take off your pajamas and put your clothes on before Nanny gets here."

Child: "Is Chase going, too?"

Dad: "Yes, Jana. You and Chase are going to spend the morning with Nanny and Poppy."

Mom: **"Daddy, did you pack the diaper bag?"**

Dad: "It's all set. Come on, Jana, let's change your clothes."

Child: "Daddy, I don't want to wear that one. I want to wear the red one."

Dad: "This is fine."

Child: "Daddy, I want to wear the bear."

Dad: "Jana, you can wear either this one or that one. You choose."

Child: "OK, Daddy. I want the purple one."

Dad: "Let's get your shoes on."

Child: "I want my sneakers."

Dad: "That's fine. Let's put your sneakers on. Nanny will be here in a few minutes."

21st-Century Dad

Mom: "Honey, is Chase ready to go?"

Dad: "You better check his diaper again."

Mom: "Come on, little man. Let's get you a new diaper."

7:15 a.m.

Dad: "Honey, your Mom is here. I'm loading up Jana."

Mom: "Oh no, she needs a new diaper. [first poop diaper of the day]
Be right there. Mom, if you need anything just give us a call."

Dad: "See you later, angel."

Child: "Bye, Daddy."

Mom: "Honey, could you load up Chase? I have to finish putting on my make-up and load up the breast pump."

Dad: "Sure. See you later kids, and thank you, Nanny. Bye-Bye."

7:30 a.m.

Mom: "Honey, could you please put the pump in the car? I have so much to carry."

Dad: "Relax!"

Mom: "You relax. All you have to do today is go to work like normal. I have to pump in 2 hours and then run to Mom's after work to pick up the kids, feed Chase and then make a plan for dinner. What time will you be home?"

Dad: "I will be home at 5:00 pm."

Mom: "Honey, I'm sorry I snapped at you but last night was a killer. I need more than 4 hours of sleep."

Dad: "Me too, but that's the way it is for the next few weeks."

Mom: "I love you, Honey."

Dad: "I love you, too. See you this afternoon."

9:30 a.m. – Call to Nanny.

Mom: "How are the kids?"

Nanny: "They're fine. How are you?"

Mom: "I'm pumping milk in my office and then I have to teach a class."

| 10:30 a.m. |— Dad receives a call from Mom.

Mom: "Hi, Honey. How's your day?"

Dad: "We're busy, but I'll be home by 5 p.m. See you then."

| 5:00 p.m. |– Dad comes home, and both parents begin fixing the meal.

| 5:30 p.m. |

Dad: "Jana, let's clean your room!"

Child: "OK, Daddy."

Dad: "I have to make dinner so we can eat. When you're done, you can watch TV until we eat." [**this is the first time the TV was on all day**]

| 6:30 p.m. |— After a quick dinner, Mom begins feeding the baby.

Mom: **"Honey, could you change Chase and give both kids a bath? I have to finish the lesson plans for tomorrow."**

Dad: "Sure."

Mom: **"I'll get the stuff."**

Dad: "Jana, would you like to help Daddy give Chase a bath?"

Child: "OK, Daddy."

Dad: "After we are done with Chase, you can have your bath."

| 7:30 p.m. |— Chase is next to Mom in the bouncer, and Dad starts the bath for Jana. After a few minutes Chase is placed in the crib.

| 8:30 p.m. |— Following the bath and a clean pair of pajamas, Jana and Dad play on the floor and then the entire family sits down to watch the Discovery channel. We share a snack and remind Jana that bedtime is around the corner.

| 9:00 p.m. |— Mom retrieves Chase from the bed and resumes the feeding schedule.

Mom: **"Honey, remember to brush Jana's teeth before she goes to bed."**

Dad: "OK. Jana, Let's brush your teeth. Time to go to sleep, little girl."

Child: "I'm big."

Dad: "Let's say good night to Mom and go say our prayers."

21st-Century Dad

[We recite the Lord's prayer and bless all family members]

Dad: "Jana, see you tomorrow."

Child: "Daddy, you go. I wake up when the sun comes out."

Dad: "That's right. Good night, my angel."

9:30 p.m.

Mom: **"Honey, can you burp the baby, change his diaper and put him to bed before you watch the basketball game?"**

Dad: "Sure."

11:15 p.m. — After Sports Center highlights, Dad goes to bed.

1:30 a.m. — Chase wakes up screaming.

Mom: **"Honey, can you get the baby?"**

Dad: "Sure. How many hours was it?"

Mom: **"Four."**

Dad: "That's not so bad. Here's the baby, which side first?" [After retrieving the baby, Dad uses the rest room but is so tired he has to sit to pee]

Mom: **"Honey, could you change the baby and put him down?"** [Jana walks in the room]

Child: "Daddy, hold me."

Dad: "Jana, it's not time to wake up yet."

Child: "I want to sleep with you."

Mom: **"Remember what the doctor said. If she sleeps with us now, she will for the next 2 years."**

Dad: "Jana, let's go to your big-girl bed."

Child: "OK, Daddy. You sleep with me?"

Dad: "Just for a minute."

4:30 a.m. — Chase wakes up for the second feeding of the evening. This time, however, he does not want to go back to sleep and ends up screaming until 5:30 a.m. Just as Mom and Dad fall to sleep, the 6:00 a.m. alarm goes off and we start the process all over again.

This depiction represents an actual day in my Family and probably parallels many households with young children and a newborn. Of course, your day will certainly be different, but many of the same circumstances will arise in your lives. If your Family uses a day-care facility or your job is not flexible, your day may be even more involved and require additional drop-off and pick-up time for the sitter.

21st-Century Dad

Precious Experiences

Becoming a Dad is the best experience I have ever had. Marriage is certainly excellent, graduation was fulfilling and other personal accomplishments have been rewarding. But to be a Dad is awesome.

Knowing that Mom and this beautiful Baby are looking to you for guidance is incredible. Until you actually have a child of your own — be it adopted or blood related – you will not understand the indescribable feeling you have when you hold and nurture your Baby.

Life is precious, and the little things in life are what you hope to share with your Child. I can't wait until Mom and I take our daughter and son to an amusement park. I can't wait until my children have their first feeling of success. I can't wait to swim in the ocean with my kids or drive across country with them on a family vacation. There are so many experiences yet to come.

I'd like to close with a few experiences I have treasured to date:

- Dancing with my little girl in the living room (she doesn't care that I can't dance)
- Helping my little girl feed a cracker to a giraffe (she thinks Dad is so brave)
- Showing my little boy how to hit the movable toys mounted on his bouncer (he was only 2 months old)
- Seeing my little boy squirt Mom and my mother-in-law during a diaper change
- Snuggling with my entire Family on the couch on a Friday night and being happy with a children's movie

Most likely you will experience many of the topics I have discussed, but most of all I hope you enjoy becoming a Dad as much as I have. 21st-Century Dads arrive on the scene every day, so welcome them to the club and help them along. Dad, best of luck to you on your adventure.

Appendix A

The following items have been classified as a "Must" however, they are not listed in a priority order.

Changing table - If you want to have a place to store all changing supplies (diapers, wipes, lotions, alcohol, swabs) and do not want to develop a sore back, a changing table is critical. Bending over a crib and changing Baby on the counter, on the bed or on the floor is possible. However, when you change 15-18 diapers a day during the first six months and at least 8 diapers a day for two years, a central location is extremely helpful. This item could be purchased at a neighborhood garage sale and then a new pad can be put on it.

> Time used: From birth through potty training
> Cost ($60 - $100)

Changing-table pad - A plastic pad should be used on top of the changing table. This pad is easy to clean and provides a sanitary surface for your Child.

> Time used: From birth through potty training
> Cost ($4 - $20)

Crib - The crib does not have to be new and elaborate to be effective. However, if you purchase or receive a crib as a gift, make sure the bars are no more than 2 inches apart. This safety feature could prevent your Child from becoming stuck between the bars when she is older. The crib should be adjustable to allow you to raise and lower the mattress and side rail. This can be done by removing the set screw on all four corner supports and adjusting the height to meet your needs. When Baby is first born you should have the crib set on the highest level and then adjust accordingly as Baby matures and begins to crawl and stand. If you obtain a "used crib" you may feel more comfortable purchasing a new mattress and mattress liner to ensure cleanliness for your Child. The location of the crib should be away from stairs or uneven surfaces in the home, away from ventilation ducts that might blow hot/cold air toward the Child and away from windows that might expose Baby to drafts and unwanted sunlight.

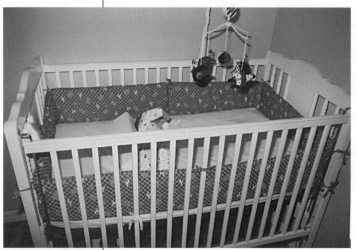

The crib should also be in a controlled environment free from throwing of objects by siblings or siblings climbing in when you are not there.

> Time used: From birth until you move the Child to a toddler bed (Approx 2 years)
>
> Cost: ($100 - $500)

Mattress, mattress cover/liner/pad - Since newborns need to be protected from exposure to unnecessary germs and nurtured in a clean environment, you should consider purchasing a new mattress rather than borrowing one or buying one from a garage sale. The mattress cover/liner/pad should also be purchased new to ensure that germs, mildew and dust do not affect your Child. A mattress cover can save endless hours of scrubbing and hence unnecessary arguments with your wife. Undoubtedly, you will be asked to scrub the pee and puke stains at the most inconvenient times.

> Time used: From birth until you move the Child to a toddler bed (Approx 2 years)
>
> Cost: ($52 - $115)

Sheets and blankets - Similar to the mattress cover/liner/pad, sheets are necessary to keep the Child free from germs and to provide warmth to the newborn. The issue here is the number of sheets you really need versus the number of sheets Mom says you need because they are cute and match the room. Babies are high-maintenance. If you do not like to wash daily, you may want to consider purchasing a few sets of sheets. As far as the number of blankets needed, you will need to have at least two or three receiving blankets, a thin warm-weather blanket and a heavy cold-weather blanket. Since blankets become soiled or misplaced regularly, it is wise to have a few extras on hand. Nevertheless, having a different color and style for each day of the week is a personal decision only you and Mom can make.

Time used: From birth until you move the Child to a toddler bed (Approx 2 years)

Cost: ($8 - $15)

Stroller, umbrella - An umbrella stroller is a super light- weight, easy-to-carry, mode of transportation for your Child. The umbrella stroller does not allow for an adjustment of the handle, cannot venture through difficult terrain and does  not carry much more than the Child. Nevertheless, the umbrella stroller is simple to fold, easy to carry and a great way to keep your Child in check while you are shopping.

Time used: From 2 months until the Child is too big for the stroller (Up to 4 years)

Costs: ($25 - $30)

Stroller, full-size - A full-size stroller provides you the opportunity to transport diaper bags and shopping bags all at the same time. When considering a stroller, look for products that include these features: seat belt, adjustable handle, two carrying satchels, wheel brakes, a movable back rest that allows the Child to lie down or sit up, and wheels appropriate for your anticipated use. If the terrain is rough be sure to buy a rugged stroller with large knobby wheels. If use is limited to visits to the mall, then traditional small-sized wheels will suffice. The unit should be easy to fold, lightweight, durable and easy to clean. Additional features might include a sun visor, safety padding or the ability to convert into a carriage/stroller.

> Time used: From as soon as you are home from the hospital until your Child no longer wants to use the stroller (Up to 4 years)
>
> Costs: ($40 - $160)

Sunscreen - Sunscreen (advanced block) is mandatory for all children (6 months and older) who are exposed to the sun. Dermatologists have stated that the first few sunburns on humans influence the probability of contracting skin cancer. Therefore, all Parents should apply sunscreen to their children whenever they might be exposed to the sun.

> Time used: From 6 months through adult life
>
> Costs: ($7 - $15)

Lotion - Lotion is necessary to keep Baby's skin moist and soft. Newborns and young babies need moisturizers as much as or more than adults. Infants with sensitive skin should be given only lotions recommended by their physician.

> Time used: From birth through adult life
>
> Costs: ($2 - $14)

Diapers - Diapers in the 21st century may be disposable or cloth. However, most people choose disposable. Some people use cloth diapers because their Child is allergic to the plastic disposable diaper. Cloth diaper users may investigate utilizing a diaper service to launder and deliver the clean diapers. Disposable diapers are available in several qualities and price ranges, with the name brands being the most popular choice for most families. Some Parents will use nothing but name brands. But when you change about 18 diapers a day, the more expensive brands can really affect the budget. If your Baby has sensitive skin, the generic diaper may not be possible but, more than likely, Baby will be able to use the local store brand. The more expensive name-brand diapers do absorb moisture better than the cheaper store brands. But if you change Baby frequently, they really are not necessary. A cloth diaper may serve a dual purpose as a burp cloth.

> Time used: From birth until you are able to potty train the Child (Approx 2 - 3.5 years)
>
> Costs: ($20 - $60/month)

Diaper bags - A Diaper bag is necessary to carry all the items you will need to change or care for Baby. Some Parents purchase a super-deluxe bag while others use the generic bag provided by the hospital. I would recommend having both the large deluxe bag for long trips or lengthy stays and the small generic bag for trips to the grocery store or other short outings. A deluxe bag will come equipped with several interior compartments (for wet and dry storage) 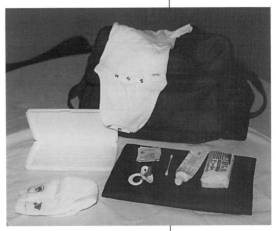 and at least two exterior pockets for holding drink cups and snack dispensers. The deluxe bag should come with a changing pad, an interior storage compartment for supplies and also be equipped with a strap and handles. The generic bag has only one compartment. Diaper bags come in hundreds of colors, styles, types of material and price ranges, so be sure to shop around.

> Time used: From birth until the Child is potty trained and no longer needs a bib (Approx 3 - 4 years)
>
> Costs: ($10 - $35)

Petroleum jelly - Physicians recommend petroleum jelly to help provide protection for the penis on newly circumcised boys. It may also be used for diaper rash, but other medicated creams are preferred by many Parents.

> Time used: From birth through adult life
>
> Costs: ($2 - $3)

Rubbing alcohol, alcohol wipes and swabs - Rubbing alcohol and swabs are necessary to clean the umbilical cord stump on the newborn and should be on hand at least until the stump falls off. At home you may prefer to use a plastic bottle of rubbing alcohol, but out in public a sealed alcohol wipe may prove to be more convenient.

Time used: From birth through adult life

Costs: ($1 - $2)

Diaper-rash cream - There are several name-brand and generic diaper-rash creams to choose from, but undoubtedly, Baby will eventually need a medicated cream to help heal advanced diaper rash.

Time used: From birth through potty training (Approx 2 - 3.5 years)

Costs: ($2 - $4)

Bathing items (towel, washcloth) - A few baby washcloths and towels are necessary to bathe Baby and keep you from doing wash every day. Baby towels are softer than the traditional adult towel, and most Baby towels have a pocket in the corner to help cover Baby's wet head.

Time used: From birth until you choose to use adult towels (Approx 1 - 2 years)

Costs: ($6 - $10)

Portable bathtub - Several plastic tubs designed for infant bathing will meet Baby's bathing needs. Most tubs are self-contained and have a foam pad to protect Baby from slipping during the bath. Others have a separate insert to serve the same purpose. Many Parents purchase a plastic tub and also purchase a foam pad to place in the kitchen sink when bathing the newborn. This foam pad is inexpensive ($4) and may be useful in your situation. Nevertheless, you will eventually need a bathing station larger than your sink when Baby is a few months old. A portable plastic tub can also be placed in the shower and requires less preparation time to fill and clean than a traditional bathtub.

Time used: From birth until you move Baby to the large tub (Approx 1 year)

Costs: ($10 - $20)

Infant car seat - An approved car seat is necessary to transport Baby. Hospital staff will not let you take Baby home if your car is not equipped with an approved seat. Most Parents use a portable infant seat during the first 10 months and then switch to a larger seat that will remain in the car. The infant seat doubles as a carrier for Baby when you are on the go and need a safe place for the Child. These items are manufactured in several styles and come in a variety of colors. You will need to determine if your infant car seat will come with a carrying handle and, if so, what style you prefer. Additionally, some seats come with protective pads that keep Baby's head stabilized while others do not. Further-

more, a terry-cloth pad can be added to protect Baby's neck and collarbones from the nylon straps holding him in.

Time used: From birth until you move Baby to the toddler seat (Approx 1 year)

Costs: ($40 - $60)

Toddler car seat - Although you will not need to purchase a toddler car seat until your Child is old enough to safely support her head and face the front of the vehicle, eventually you will need one. Toddler car seats come in a variety of styles and have several

safety features. Just be sure to use a seat that provides plenty of padding, has adjustable straps, is easily secured and easy to use. Again, be sure your seat has a terry-cloth pad on each strap to protect your Child's face.

Time used: From 1 year through toddler (Approx 3 years)

Costs: ($40 - $85)

Car Seats:

Left: for children up to 1 year or 20 pounds.

Middle: for children up to 40 pounds.

Right: for children 30-60 pounds.

See manufacturer's instructions.

Stain remover and bleach - A top-quality stain remover is necessary to maintain the quality and appearance of the clothes your Child will wear. Dirty diapers undoubtedly leak, babies spit up and spills are normal in a household with children.

> Time used: From birth through adult life
>
> Costs: ($4 - $7)

Bib - A flexible and easy-to-clean bib is necessary in the home and in the diaper bag. Plastic bibs with snaps, Velcro or tie strings and food-catching pockets are the best. They come in a variety of colors, materials and sizes for each stage of development. The extra-large over-the-shoulder bib is excellent when the Child begins to eat by himself.

> Time used: From birth (drool and spit-up) through toddler (Approx 3 years)
>
> Costs: ($2 - $8)

Clothes - Typical clothing for newborns includes undergarments, hats, sleepers, shoes, socks and unisex outfits. Specialty items or clothes made specifically for boys or girls are "Must" items, but quality, quantity and style are based upon Parents' desires.

> Time used: From birth until Baby grows out of the item (anywhere from 2 months to 1 year)
>
> Costs: vary

Baby shampoo - A gentle, no tear shampoo made for babies is necessary for bath time.

> Time used: From birth through toddler (Approx 3 years)
>
> Costs: ($2 - $8)

Baby soap - A hypoallergenic unscented soap is needed to protect Baby's skin during bath time.

> Time used: From birth through toddler (Approx 3 years)
>
> Costs: ($2 - $8)

Thermometer (found in a nurse kit) - A mercury human thermometer or an electronic human thermometer is needed to take Baby's temperature. If you consider an electronic machine similar to the one in the doctor's office, you will need to pay more than a hundred dollars to guarantee an accurate reading. Consult with your doctor. A typical nurse kit provides a thermometer, suction syringe and nail clippers.

Time used: From birth through adult life

Costs: ($8 - $10)

Burp cloth - Could be a cloth diaper or a soft cloth made for wiping drool and spit-up from Baby's face.

Time used: From birth through toddler (Approx 3 years)

Costs: ($3 - $5)

Wet wipes - Although I would not recommend changing a diaper without the handy-dandy wet wipe, it really is not necessary if Parents are willing to use a clean, warm washcloth each time they change a diaper. Most Parents prefer the pre-packaged wet wipes available on the market. Again, just like the varying quality of diapers, if Baby has sensitive skin the more expensive wipes are recommended. If Baby does not have sensitive skin, the generic brand will save you money.

Time used: From birth through adult life

Costs: ($3 - $6)

21st-
Century
Dad

Appendix B

These items are not mandatory but could be considered "Highly useful":

Wet-wipe warmer - An electric wet-wipe warmer keeps the wipes warm to the touch at all times. (Note: Ours was recalled because of an electrical defect.)

> Time used: From birth through potty training but most Parents use them only for small Babies. (Approx 2 - 3.5 years)
>
> Costs: ($12 - $22)

Portable crib - Some manufacturers make portable cribs that may be used for day visits and overnight travel. This item serves as a bed and also converts into a playpen when the Child becomes mobile. If your Family is on the go, a portable crib is extremely useful but would probably be considered a frivolous expense to Parents who never travel.

> Time used: From birth through toddler (Approx 2 years)
>
> Cost: ($80 - $120)

Mobiles - Mobiles are designed for several reasons but are usually purchased to help Baby track movement, as well as to calm and relax Baby prior to bedtime. Certainly, mobiles look nice. But their primary purpose goes beyond playing music and comforting Baby. Parents should be cautioned that using a mobile too frequently may impair Baby's ability to sleep in unfamiliar locations.

> Time used: From birth until Baby can sit up (because he might grab it and hurt himself) (Approx 9 months)
>
> Costs: ($20 - $80)

Crib side pads/quilt - Pads prevent Baby from having her leg or arm caught between crib rails. Additionally, pads protect Baby from bruises suffered by bumping up against the rails. Towels, blankets or pillows are not recommended because Baby could be suffocated by them.

> Time used: From birth until Baby stands on them to get out of the crib (Up to 1 year)
>
> Costs: ($40 - $60)

Baby stabilizers - Padded stabilizers help hold Baby in place while he sleeps. The purpose of the pads is to stabilize and retain Baby in the sleeping position recommended by most physicians.

> Time used: From birth until Baby rolls over (Approx 3 months)
>
> Costs: ($15 - $17)

Diaper stacker - Diaper stackers are usually hung on the side of the crib or the changing table. The stacker makes changing a diaper a bit more convenient because the diaper is easily accessible with one hand while you hold Baby with the other.

> Time used: From birth through potty training (Approx 2 - 3.5 years)
>
> Costs: ($10 - $30)

Bouncers - Bouncers provide a safe alternative to the crib, infant seat or swing and are useful if you want to keep an eye on Baby while you perform chores around the house. The bouncer also provides an environment for the Child to reach for or bat items attached to the unit.

> Time used: From birth through 6 months
>
> Costs: ($20 - $40)

Sling - Baby slings are useful because they allow Mom to carry and feed Baby and still have the use of her hands. The Baby-carrying sling goes over one shoulder and around the back of the other, thus creating a hammock for Baby. Slings come in a variety of colors and materials, with the better-designed slings providing more comfort than the cheaper versions.

Time used: From birth through 8 - 10 months

Costs: ($20 - $50)

Vaporizer - Vaporizers add moisture to the air to help the congested Baby breathe. If your Child is susceptible to colds, bronchitis or pneumonia, a vaporizer may become a must in your Family.

Time used: From birth through adult life

Costs: ($12 - $30)

Automatic baby swing - Infant swings are crank- or battery-powered, lightweight and portable. They are equipped with a safety belt and a pad to protect Baby and serve many useful purposes. Most of all, Parents love them because they allow Baby to sit up and watch what is going on while you work around the house. Swings also provide a calming effect on Babies who enjoy swinging or swaying.

Time used: From 2 weeks through 9 months

Costs: ($40 - $120)

Pacifier - A pacifier is a device designed to satisfy the natural sucking reflex all Babies have. Although some Parents believe a pacifier is a crutch and unnecessary, others would pay several thousand dollars for a pacifier if it helped to comfort and quiet their Child. Some researchers have suggested that pacifiers help educate the tongue in preparation for speech. If you choose to use a pacifier, keep an eye on the rubber component to make sure it is replaced before it wears out or rips, thus ensuring the safety of your Child.

Time used: Usually from birth through 1 year, yet some kids will use a pacifier for up to 4 years, if allowed

Costs: ($1 - $3)

21st-Century Dad

Baby monitor - A baby monitor provides audio link between you and Baby when Baby is sleeping. Whether you are across the house, upstairs or in the garage, this device enables you to hear Baby's cry from a distant location. Some Parents would never go out of the room without turning on the baby monitor, while others believe the monitor is unnecessary and influences their own sleeping patterns. If you are a light sleeper, you will hear every sound Baby makes throughout the night. As Baby approaches toddler age, the monitor may be useful to you if you want to hear the Child in another room.

> Time used: From birth through toddler (Approx 3 years)
> Costs: ($20 - $150)

Activity board for crib -A multi-station activity board that attaches to the crib or playpen provides several tasks for the Child to test her abilities and keep her occupied. Activity boards are educational and challenge the Child to push, pull, roll, spin, turn and click the various apparatus.

> Time used: From 6 months through 2 years
> Costs: ($10 - $25)

Chest/back carrier - If you enjoy walking and want to be free of a stroller (good for nature walks), a chest/back carrier that attaches to the adult like a backpack is useful.

> Time used: From 2 months through 11 months (Approx 1.5 years)
> Costs: ($15 - $80)

Supplementary rearview auto mirror - A stick-on rearview mirror is comforting to you because you can see Baby while you drive. Remember, Baby is facing the rear of the vehicle during those early months because of his weak neck.

> Time used: From birth through toddler (Approx 3 years)
> Costs: ($3 - $5)

Sunshade - A clip-on shade you suction to the window can keep the sun off Baby while you drive. In most cases a rear and side shade are necessary to complete the task.

Time used: From birth through adult life

Costs: ($5 - $7)

Medical supplies - Your doctor will recommend what is best for you to administer, but over-the-counter treatments are available and can be helpful in times of illness (acetaminophen, ibuprofen, saltwater drops, bulb syringe, eucalyptus rub).

Time used: From birth through adult life

Costs: ($4 - $8 each)

Simethicone anti-gas drops - To help reduce gas bubbles in Baby's stomach, you may consider using infant anti-gas drops. The active ingredient simethicone can be purchased in name-brand products or as a generic item. (Consult with your doctor before you use the drops.)

Time used: From birth through adult life

Costs: ($4 - $8)

Camera - Allows you to capture the precious experiences of your growing Child.

Time used: From birth through adult life

Costs: ($5 - $500+)

Video recorder - Allows you to capture the precious experiences of your growing Child.

Time used: From birth through adult life

Costs: ($350 - $600+)

21st-Century Dad

Appendix C

Here's a list of diaper bag contents you need to have packed when you leave for the day.

A carefully organized diaper bag can be the difference between an enjoyable outing and a miserable day. Before you leave the house, be sure to double-check the contents and have all compartments stocked because you never know when the unexpected will occur. Items Mom and I have found to be helpful include:

- Change of clothes
  Undershirt
  New shirt top
  New bottom (must match)
  Extra blanket
- Diapers
- Wet wipes
- Alcohol swab
- Bib
- Burp cloth
- Pacifier

When Baby becomes a toddler, you may need:

- Jacket or sweater for time of year
- Non-spill drink cup with a drink
- Snack cup with snacks
- Hair ties or barrettes for girls

21st-
Century
Dad

Glossary

Amniocentesis
Sometimes called an "amnio," this minor surgical diagnostic test allows the doctor to obtain a sample of the amniotic fluid. The amniotic fluid is then analyzed to look for genetic characteristics of Baby or to check on the maturity of the unborn Baby's lungs. Amniocentesis is a common way to obtain material for genetic and other testing of the Baby. The doctor inserts a long, thin, hollow needle through Mom's abdomen into the uterus and amniotic fluid. Usually the doctor uses ultrasound imaging to guide the needle. The small amount of fluid removed should not affect Baby. The risk of complications from the procedure is low, but, as with any procedure, complications can occur. Be sure to consult with your doctor before the procedure is performed.

amniotic fluid
Fluid inside the membrane that forms a sac around the embryo and later the fetus. The fetus and the placenta produce the amniotic fluid. This buoyant fluid helps the fetus grow uniformly, helps the bones and muscles develop and allows Baby to move within the uterus. Babies breathe this fluid in and out of their lungs in the womb, helping the lungs to grow as well.

breast pump
A mechanical device that pumps breast milk from the breast so that it can be stored for later consumption by Baby. There are both manually operated and electrically operated pumps. The electric pump is far easier and more likely to maintain the flow of milk.

C-section
Abbreviation for Cesarean section.

Cesarean section

Delivery of Baby through an incision in the abdominal and uterine walls when delivery through the birth canal is impossible or dangerous. This procedure was performed as early as 715 BC and can be lifesaving for both Baby and Mom in certain situations.

colic

Persistent, inconsolable crying, especially in the evening. Colic is a common problem that affects 6-13% of all Babies. Colicky Babies cry for an average of four hours a day, enough to irritate even the most loving Parent.

dilation

Opening up, enlargement of a tubular structure. This usually refers to the cervical dilation that occurs during labor. The opening of the cervix must go from essentially 0 centimeters to about 10 centimeters, the usual size required for Baby to pass through the cervix, which forms part of the birth canal. The first stage of labor is that part of labor during which the cervix dilates up to 10 cm or is completely dilated. This usually takes several hours and is shorter with subsequent pregnancies.

episiotomy

A minor surgical procedure that widens the birth canal by cutting the vaginal opening. Episiotomy is performed to prevent the jagged, less controlled tearing of the tissue during the stretching associated with delivery.

mastitis

Inflammation of the breast, usually caused by infection.

midwife

Midwives help Moms with all stages of pregnancy and delivery. They provide prenatal care, attend and help with the birth process, provide post-partum care, and some provide routine gynecological services.

OB

Abbreviation for obstetrician or obstetrics.

obstetrician
These doctors receive at least four years of specialty training in the provision of women's health services. This includes pregnancy, delivering babies, postnatal care and women's health issues throughout life.

pacifier
A usually nipple-shaped device for Babies to suck on.

pediatrician
Specialists in pediatrics spend at least three years after medical school studying children's health problems. Many devote additional years to subspecialize in a particular area of pediatrics such as heart, lung or endocrine problems.

perinatal
Refers to the time period after the 28th week of gestation and ending the first week after birth. Some sources extend the perinatal period until the fourth week after birth.

placenta
Organ within the uterus that provides communication between Mom and fetus through the umbilical cord. The placenta enables oxygen and nutrients to pass from Mom's blood to the fetus. It also eliminates carbon dioxide and waste products from Baby by passing them to Mom, who excretes them with her liver, kidneys or lungs. It is a disk-shaped organ and at term weighs around 500 grams.

post partum
Occurring after childbirth, or delivery.

prenatal
Occurring, existing or performed before birth.

sitz bath
A tub in which one bathes in a sitting posture.

Sudden Infant Death Syndrome

The unexplained death of an apparently healthy infant.

SIDS

SIDS (or Sudden Infant Death Syndrome) is a Parent's worst fear. An apparently healthy Baby, usually less than 12 months old, with no obvious previous or present illness is laid in bed for sleep and never awakens. Examination of the Baby's medical history, home and even an autopsy do not reveal the cause of death in true SIDS cases.

swaddling

Wrapping Baby in a blanket or cloth to restrict movement.

thrush

Yeast (Candida) infection of the mouth. This occurs most often in newborns, but can also affect older Babies who are taking antibiotics. Thrush resembles patches of cottage cheese on the inside of the cheek, tongue and the roof of the mouth. Rarely a dangerous infection, thrush can be uncomfortable for Baby. It is treated with mycostatin, a medicine given orally. Some resistant cases require additional medicine.

triage

The sorting of and allocation of treatment to patients.

trimester

A third of a pregnancy. Trimesters divide pregnancy into three 13-week periods.

ultrasound

Imaging of body parts using sound waves. Ultrasound uses sound waves that are above the range of human hearing to create an image of organs within the body. Sound waves are reflected off internal body structures and back to the ultrasound machine. The reflected sound waves are analyzed by computer and turned into pictures. This method of imaging results in less clear pictures than X-rays, CAT scans or MRI. However, there is no radiation risk with ultrasound and no confirmed adverse effects on the fetus or Mom from diagnostic ultrasound examinations in pregnancy.

21st-Century
Dad

Dr. Douglas DeMichele and Family
wife Pam, daughter Jana and son Chase

About the Author

Dr. DeMichele has a doctorate degree in Educational Leadership from the University of Florida and has been employed as a university administrator for fourteen years. He is actively involved in rearing his children and believes the best gift you can give your Family is your undivided attention. Hope you enjoy the book!